TRUST THE JOURNEY EMBRACE THE PROCESS

SCOTT W. BONDS

Trust the Journey Embrace the Process

© 2019 Scott W. Bonds

All rights reserved

Table of Contents

COPYRIGHT INFORMATION............ ERROR! BOOKMARK NOT DEFINED.

YEAR OF PUBLICATION ERROR! BOOKMARK NOT DEFINED.

ACKNOWLEDGEMENTS 5

CHAPTER 1: FINDING MY PATH 15

CHAPTER 2: WHAT MADE ME WANT TO DO HAIR? 23

CHAPTER 3: MY FIRST SALON EXPERIENCE 37

CHAPTER 4: A WHOLE NEW WORLD AWAITS ME 43

CHAPTER 5: BEGINNING TO BUILD MY DREAM 51

CHAPTER 6: ON TO THE NEXT THING! (THE RIGHT ANGLE) 61

CHAPTER 7: THE CHANGE TO COME 73

CHAPTER 8: LESSONS LEARNED 77

CHAPTER 9: DOWN… BUT NOT OUT. 89

CHAPTER 10: THE EVOLUTION OF THE INDUSTRY SALON STUDIO 96

CHAPTER 11: DIVAS, EGOS, AND ATTITUDES 105

CHAPTER 12: THE STORM BEFORE THE CALM 113

CHAPTER 13: THE GREATEST MIRACLE 119

CHAPTER 14: REST AND RECOVERY 125

CHAPTER 15: WHEN THE PIECES FALL IN PLACE 129

CHAPTER 16: WHAT YOU DON'T SEE… 135

CHAPTER 17: EVERYTHING IS PURPOSEFUL, NOTHING HAPPENS BY COINCIDENCE. 141

CHAPTER 18: HOW MUCH IS YOUR FREEDOM WORTH TO YOU? 149

CHAPTER 19: I HAVE EVERYTHING I NEED, TO SUCCEED 153

EPILOGUE 157

Acknowledgements

I would like to acknowledge a few people on my journey. These people would also go on to accomplish amazing things. Just to name a few, Maurice Lemons, who was one of the most admired and respected people who was a wealth of information. Micheline Washington, a top stylist doing big things to this day in the Florida area. Aphonso McGriff III, who took me under his wing, and helped me grow tremendously. Patric Bradley, who was just coming in as I was going out, but I remember seeing him one day, and I could see the fire in him and knew he would do big things as well. He too, is known internationally as is Steven P. Daniels, the hair replacement extraordinaire. Wendell Raeford, who made be practice roller setting, when I wanted nothing to do with it. Olivia Barr, Cynthia Bradger, Fredrick Parnell, Cindy Peirce, Brunetta Roberts, Ursula Dudley, Genea Dudley, Joe Dudley Jr., the First Lady, Mrs. Eunice Dudley, Terri Clawson, Betty Clawson, Clastine Poole (Covington), Larry Foote, Bonita Chapman (RIP) who was ranked as being one of the top 10 colorist in the nation, Harvey Moore, Desi Sims who became my clipper metrics team, and so many others. These were all a part of my DCU (Dudley Cosmetology University) family! Also, those who always showed me, they wanted me to win! Just to name a few, my incredible photographer Ashleigh Crawley owner of Still Shots Photography, Ike and Ayesha Oglesby, Ken and Tamika Bain, Debra Perry, Nicole Hayes, Pam Vanstory, and last but certainly not least, my wife Kelly

Bonds, my late father, Abdur Rashid Ishaq (Clyde W. Bonds) and my loving mother Dorothy L. Bonds.

Forward

Trust is defined as a reliance on the integrity, strength, ability, and surety of a person or thing; confidence.

A process is a systematic series of actions directed to some end. Do you have an end, goal or process in sight? Scott did and he shares his story with you. A story that had ups and downs, successes and failures, times when he was on top of his game and times when he hit rock bottom. There were times when the process ran into a dead-end and had to be completely redirected. He faced financial problems, family problems, salon problems, and problems with friends and associates. But through all adversity, Scott never lost hope in the process and his trust was solid enough to help him endure.

What is Your Process? Are you pursuing it, living it, nourishing it, and preparing for it? The process requires preparation, dedication, faith, hard work, motivation, drive and determination. Throughout the process you may have to make adjustments, changes or even a total redirection but, "Don't Give Up" TRUST THE PROCESS.

Following the process required Scott to reinvent himself and discover hidden inner strengths that were not as recognized as his hairstyling abilities. Again, he is reinventing himself as an author and discussion panel host.

This book is not just for cosmetologists, even though it is authored by a cosmetologist. Trust the Process will motivate, encourage, re-energize and hopefully help you to identify your process and the confidence to "Trust the Process."

Scott, I love you like a son. May blessings surround you as you follow the process.

Boz....
Morris "Boz" Boswell
Cosmetology Educator/Cosmetology Industry Leader

Preface

Whenever I think about writing my story and the journey I've traveled in this great profession of cosmetology, I've struggled with how transparent I should be. It is my hope as well as my belief that my journey will help someone to fight a little harder when going through the many different adversity's life brings. Sharing is important to me, especially when speaking to the youth. On the occasions where I have had the opportunity to speak to inner city kids, I always let them know it is my intention to include myself. Never do I want to make people feel as if I am judging. I emphasize once being their age and experiencing very similar things. The outline of my thinking when bearing my story is not limited to just young men and women. I do the same when speaking to my peers. I intentionally like to contribute portions of my life. I like to interact rather than talk at them. For this reason, I've coined myself a Motivational Conversationalist.

There are four sayings that have remained with me. "What doesn't kill you, makes you stronger." "Everything must change." "Nothing ever lasts forever." Lastly, "The main problem with being strong is no one ever checks to see how you are doing." During my difficult transitions in life, here is the best way I can describe to you how I felt. It was as if I was a part of a big gathering amongst all my peers. Everyone was drinking wine, dancing, and simply appeared

to be having a good time. I, however, was hanging on the edge of a cliff just beneath their feet, and not even holding on with all ten fingers. From time to time, someone might notice me there hanging, but they would look down, see me, and say to themselves, "Oh, that's Scott, no need to worry about him. He's always good." To add injury to insult, someone might even step on my fingers, just to see how much longer I could hold on. Unbeknownst to them, the day finally came where I simply couldn't hang on any longer. I was forced to let go and fly strictly on faith!

As a "human becoming," as my brother Alphonso McGriff III, author of *The Book of Abe* says, you should continuously evolve to a higher consciousness. You see, I have this philosophy. Somewhere in life God sends you your own personal storm. You don't get to choose what your storm may be. You don't get to choose when your storm hits. It may be the death of a loved one, the heartbreak of all heartbreaks in your personal relationship, maybe even bankruptcy and you lose everything you've ever attained. Whatever the case, all you can do is decide how you will weather this storm of life. The way you choose to handle it are the final stages of God molding you into the person that you will be for a great remainder of your life. At my worst, I knew that whatever my actions would be, there would be a consequence or a reward shortly thereafter.

One bad decision could have caused me to easily become that guy holding a sign at the intersection of the highway asking for help. I also knew that most people would tell the story of my life from their own prospective and keep it moving. These pervasive thoughts had me imagining conversations going something like this. "See that dude right there?" (as you come to a stop light). "Yeah, the man holding the sign. He used to be the man back in the day. He had some of the nicest salons anywhere in this area and was always well dressed. Then, all of a sudden, he just fell apart and went crazy," and they would drive on as the light turned green.

I've been a hair stylist for the better part of 30 years now. When I tell you time really flies, BELIEVE ME. I have been asked, "What made you want to do hair?" more than any single question throughout my career. I will share my journey from the very beginning, as well as my evolution as a stylist, a business man, and a man. Though I've been pretty successful by most people's standards, all the successes only came as I learned from my failures. I hope by sharing and being transparent as possible, I will be able to help someone make better choices, as well as inspire others in their journey and pursuit of entrepreneurship.

People typically see the end result of the many sacrifices of successful people. They see the nice cars, beautiful homes, and other material things that make people appear to be successful, but it is the journey that is by far more important and worthy to be studied than anything else. Many are trying to build first generation wealth. Most of us

have a desire to be successful, but more often than not, we don't have any real guidance, so typically, we have to learn as we go. Those who are fortunate enough to be of second-generation wealth, usually have much more guidance, access and knowledge of the resources necessary to continue on the path of success. I once had a client of mine who is a successful doctor explain to me that organizations like Jack and Jill, as well as other "secret societies", are designed to share information and opportunities amongst the elite. I believe these type of private groups do many good things with good intent, but I believe information should be shared with ALL people, not just the well to do. Personally, I've always tried to stay away from groups and organizations that cause more separation amongst people. I've tried to share whatever I know with any person that may be helpful.

  It has also been my experience that very successful people typically won't just give you money because they believe in you or your vision, but they will recommend books for you to read and study. The one thing many of us miss is that to break the cycle of poverty, someone at some point must make the necessary sacrifices that will benefit the next generation. As simple as you would think this is, it's really not so simple for most of us. Becoming a successful entrepreneur is like pledging a fraternity or sorority. Many things that happen along the pledge process will not be immediately understood and will sometimes be painful. However, somewhere during this journey, you will learn to trust the process, and embrace the journey.

When we work hard, we feel like we deserve to shine. I can't tell you how many times I've heard someone say, "I deserve this. I work hard." The problem is that most of what we feel we deserve ends up being a depreciating asset. For example, when I had a $22,000 equity line of credit, back in the early 90's, it would have been ideal for me to have purchased a building in the downtown area where I live, rather than buy a brand new Lexus at that time. It wasn't that I didn't deserve the Lexus, but a building I looked at in 1993 that was selling for $150,000 is now worth about $500,000 today. My 98' Lexus is almost worth nothing now. I do, however, have great memories and a few nostalgic pictures that have absolutely no cash value. I would learn similar lessons in entrepreneurship and walking in your passion.

I think back to when I graduated high school and hearing people talk about others they knew who got jobs that were not necessarily considered prestigious, such as postal workers, fireman, etc. Though these career paths were not viewed as big deal then, if they stayed the course, these same people would comfortably retire at a young age, while many entrepreneurs miss the significance in planning for retirement early on and find themselves later playing catch up. In addition to planning for the future, it is also imperative to choose something you are truly passionate about and figure out how to make it profitable, as many of us choose the path of higher education because it's what our parents want for us. While I did embrace wisdom, I also learned early on to do what was best for me.

When a person makes the decision to pursue the life and **journey** of an entrepreneur, you will find that you will learn lessons that cannot be taught in any class room or on any college campus. Surprisingly enough, and more than likely, it will come with a price tag that can sometimes seem like tuition. Many times, you will hear people say how much money they feel they've wasted in the **process** of being an entrepreneur. Often, people even **quit** when they feel they are wasting money on a great idea and begin to have doubts about if they even made the right decision in the first place. True enough, part of being a smart business person, is knowing when to throw the towel in, but many times, people are actually much closer than they know, and had they pushed a little harder, for maybe just a little longer, they would've been successful. This is why when you have completely committed to be an entrepreneur, it becomes part of the very fabric of who you are and what you are made of; therefore, **you never give up**!

I have learned that some problems I have encountered have solutions that were right in front of me. Others will require much deeper thought and effort. However, there was always a way to make my vision become a reality. There was always a way to become the person I wished to be and live the life I always dreamed of. Most importantly, I had to believe in myself.

    To say the least, this journey has not been easy. This story I'm about to tell you is an outline of how I had to make decisions as an entrepreneur, as a father, as a husband, and most importantly, as a Black man navigating the road to success

1

Finding My Path

When I was twelve, I saved all the money I made doing yard work and bought my first car, a '66 Mustang. Because I was not old enough to drive, I had my brother drive it back home, and I parked it in my grandmother's backyard. I can remember the muffler falling off as we drove it home and seeing a few of my friends laughing as we passed them on the way. I knew my parents would likely not have the money to buy me a car, so my plan was to build my own car, so I would have it by the time I got my license. For the next two years, I read every book I could get my hands on that was about building engines and restoring Mustangs. Some of my friends use to tease me and tell me the kids in the neighborhood were going to make a clubhouse out of my car because it was sitting in the back yard of my grandmother's house for so long. To make a long story short, with the help of some great people, like Charlie Steward, who owned a towing business, and Larry, who owned the Citgo gas station in Montclair, NJ, I rebuilt the entire car myself and had a very nice classic hot rod by the time I got my license. In addition, these two men were the first entrepreneurs that helped shape who I would eventually become. Most of all, this experience taught me, for the very first time, how if *you can conceive something, you can achieve it!* Though there were some hard lessons I had to learn soon after, this would help shape me for future endeavors.

In high school, I played basketball and proved to play pretty well. The downfall was that I was a horrible student academically. One of the most embarrassing things to ever happen to me was the time I was put on academic suspension and had to sit out part of the basketball season. I was one, of many, stars on our team at Montclair High School, so for that reason, there was a full-page article telling the world about my failure. This was one of many lessons that I would learn that with great talent, comes great expectations, and with that comes a lot of room for disappointment, if you fall short.

Another life changing moment in my high school sports career was the time my coach, the legendary Robert (Bobby) Lester sat me on the bench for not making practice the day before a play-off game as we pursued the state championship in 1986. To add insult to injury, Morgan State

University was interested in recruiting me, and the head coach, Nathaniel Frazier, was there along with my mother who rarely was able to make my games. I was in such a zone and was so ready to play that night. It seemed like every shot I took in warm ups was dead on. At that time, I had no idea I was about to sit on the bench for the first three quarters as well as most of the fourth. As we were down just a couple of points, my teammate playing my position fouled out, and there was nobody else who could play that position.

As the crowd began chanting "put Scott in," my coach yelled down the bench to me and said," see what you do to your team when you don't show up!" As I sat there with tears streaming down my face, he motioned for me to check in the game. I had a lot to prove with less than three minutes. As the clock wound down, my teammate Erwin Sampson, stole the ball and passed it to me for a thunderous dunk on a player, Chris Gatling, who would eventually go on to have a very successful career in the NBA, and we won the game! I honestly wasn't even sure that I made it until I heard the tremendous applause from the crowd. Not only did I redeem myself, but most importantly, it taught me the importance of showing up for your team and what happens when you don't. I've continued to carry this lesson with me all my life.

      Playing sports can teach some of the same valuable lessons as being in the military. Learning your role on the team, and playing that role even when you know yo could be doing so much more, following direction, instruction, and the team work that comes along with it is very valuable. Most importantly, understanding the power of working as a team and how much more can be accomplished that way is extremely significant. I would learn more about these lessons in college.

Although I never felt like I needed to go to college to be successful, I did attend for a little more than two years. At the time, I was making pretty good money in sales, and as a result of my success with building my Mustang, all I did was spend money building hot rods, one of my first loves. Two things happened that changed my mind about going to college. The first thing was Spike Lee's movie *School Daze*. When I saw that movie, I knew I wanted to experience going to a HBCU (Historically Black College and University). I also thought to myself, if I could make the kind of money I was making without a degree, what might I be able to do with one? My girlfriend's family at that time was very big on education, but I thought I wouldn't go back to school because I was doing pretty good for someone right out of high school. I was in sales and was making about $1200 a week in 1987! With that being said,

...lfriend filled out a few college applications for me,
...rise, the first acceptance letter I received was
...lege, in Salisbury, North Carolina. I
...d to receive an acceptance letter because
...istory. When I received the acceptance

letter to Livingstone College, I was so excited! I packed up my 66' Mustang, got on Highway 85 South, and never looked back. With only $100 and the clothes on my back, I was on my way.

Though I was a horrible student in high school. In college, I was a standout student! I was on the Dean's list a few times and was admired amongst the student body and administration. The difference for me was I was now learning about many great African Americans on a campus rich with African American history. I also made a lifelong friend, Daryl Ferguson who was my roommate. He was very intelligent as well and had the same interest in fashion. I quickly learned that surrounding myself with likeminded people, or even people who knew more than me, is a great benefit. It made me strive to maintain a standard of excellence within my circle of friends.

After learning about George Washington, Abraham Lincoln, Thomas Edison, and a host of other historic figures who happen to not look like me and probably owned some of my ancestors in primary and secondary education, I was now learning about Stokley Carmichael, Imamu Baraka, Langston Hughes, Zora Neal Hurston, Walter White, Thurgood Marshall and so many others. It really helped build my self-esteem in a way that changed my life. I became so empowered, confident in who I was, and what I could accomplish. After my freshman year in college, I went back to my high school to visit and sought out Mrs. Jones who taught Black Literature. This was a class and a teacher that most students feared because she didn't play! She knew the importance of us knowing our history, and how it could empower. I needed to let her know how much I appreciated her for being so hard on the Black students in particular. Although I didn't understand it at the time, I grew to appreciate her and others like her immensely as a result of attending an HBCU.

Though my grades had improved in college due to a new sense of purpose and identity, I still didn't rely on grades to define me. From my own experience, I can bear witness it is very easy for young kids especially, to develop low self-esteem due to poor school grades and not meeting educational standards. However, everyone is not going to be a scholastic scholar and on the "A" and "B" honor roll list, but it is my belief that everyone has a gift and talent. I knew mine was in part, being an athlete and working with my hands. I just had to figure out in what capacity I was to use my gift.

During my two and a half years at Livingstone College, not only did I become a standout student, I also became one of the top barbers on campus. I remember hearing that the going price for a cut was $3.00! I had to raise the bar to at least $5. I knew then that my work was worth more, and I always needed to be paid what I believed I was worth. It reminded me of how I could never work a job for an hourly wage. As a kid cutting grass, I had a customer that wanted to pay me by the hour. It just didn't make since, because that meant that I would need to work slower to get paid more! In most cases, I just saw an hour of my time a lot more valuable to me, than it was to someone else, and I knew I would be willing to work for myself harder knowing that I would reap all of the benefits, versus allowing someone else to reap the benefit of my labor.

    In my third year of college, I transferred to another HBCU, which will remain nameless, but I absolutely hated it. By midterm of my first semester, I decided to quit. I really wanted to transfer back to Livingstone. I had a car note, and a few bills, and didn't think I would be able to maintain things in the small town of Salisbury, NC. I ended up staying in Winston Salem, NC and got a job in the mall, but being a self-taught barber, I set up shop in my apartment, complete with retail and all, and that's how I made most of my money. In my journey, I was discovering signs of my own talents and gifts. I also made sure I didn't get caught up wishing for the gifts of others. For example, a person who is gifted with a beautiful voice to sing, may want the gift of being a great athlete, and take his or her gift for granted. Walking in my own gift was my priority.

    Flashing back to when I was in the sixth grade, one of my best friends, Shawn Jennings, used to cut his own hair. I was so impressed by this, I started doing the same. After many days with a lot of mistakes on my own head, I started getting pretty good. My barbering skills were proving themselves so much so that a local legendary barber, Mr. Young, who I first met when he was with Brown and Young Barbershop on Bloomfield Ave. in my home town of Montclair, NJ (another entrepreneur), saw some of my friends, whose hair I'd been cutting, said he recognized some talent in me, and offered to train me as an apprentice. This place was actually my first jobs, as I use to hang around and sweep up the hair for the barbers, as well as go to the store for them when they needed a snack or something. Typically, they would tell me to keep the change. Mr. Young always made sure there was a lot of change left over when he asked me to go to the store for him. I always saw it as him being nice to me, but more importantly what he was doing was reinforcing "good behavior" and allowing me to learn that there can be rewards for staying on the right track. However, my response to him was I just cut hair for fun. I told him I was a business man and had plans to go in to sales on some level upon graduating high school. Fast forward, I would have never imagined cutting hair as a profession. In fact, my statement and experience in the barbershop was a self-fulfilling prophesy

2

What Made Me Want to Do Hair?

While working in the mall, I started hearing about a company, Dudley Products, that was said to be making millionaires in their sales force. Because I had great success in sales, as I mentioned earlier, I needed to find out more about this place. It was also Black owned, and that meant something to me as well. It wasn't long before I found myself speaking face to face with Mr. Joe Dudley Sr. himself. He was the co-founder along with his wife Eunice Dudley of Dudley Products Inc. This was at the height of their success, and I knew I was in the right place at the right time. I remember calling my mother with great excitement, as I told her all about this place. It was like a whole new world to me, and I was in love with it.

During my first conversation with Mr. Dudley, as I was excited to introduce myself to him as one of his future top salesmen. He told me he typically looked for college educated salesmen, but he would give me a chance. Part of the sales training was going door to door like Avon, Amway, and the company that shaped him, founded by Mr. S.B.Fuller, Fuller Products. I did this while maintaining my job in the mall for the next three months. Then, something happened that would change the rest of my life. I met this guy named Scott Byrd.

Scott came to work at the clothing store I worked at in the mall. We instantly hit it off and thought it was funny that we had the same name. Scott had a gift, and his gift helped make my gift even clearer. One day Scott told me he did women's hair on the side at his apartment and that I should stop by one day while selling products door to door. Shortly after that conversation, that's exactly what I did.

I will never forget that day. I walked upstairs to Scotts second floor apartment and knocked on the door. I heard Scott's voice say "come in." When I opened the door, there sat about seven or eight girls in a smoke filled room, and in the distance was Scott standing with a hot curling iron spinning it while blowing off the smoke. He looked at me and said, "what's up man" with much enthusiasm in his eyes. It was very clear to me at that moment, that this was his passion. This was a time when freeze curls were the hot thing in the industry, and I stood there watching Scott make hair freeze in ways I'd never seen before! I was so amazed that day. I asked Scott if I got some wigs, could he train me to do what he was doing? It was then that I realized that the company I was selling products for was also the best school of cosmetology around at that time.

I initially spoke to Mr. Dudley about how I wanted to attend cosmetology school so I could be a better, and more effective sales representative. I figured if I knew firsthand what a hair stylist needed most, I would be in the best position possible as a salesman as well, but I also saw an opportunity for me and Scott to do something together as well. Scott told me he'd never been to cosmetology school, but a big time stylist in his home town, Edna Lee Pagan, took him under her wing and taught him everything she knew. I told Scott that we should both go to school and get our license and go in to business together. His response was that he didn't have any money for school. Being the salesmen that I was, I told him to just come with me, and I'd talk us into school. The next day we went and met a woman named Olivia Barr, who was recruited by Mr. Dudley because of her and her husband's success in the industry prior to joining the Dudley organization. After a few minutes talking with her, she gave both of us our beauty school kits and told us if we really wanted to be here, simply show up for class, and we would find a way to pay for it. I talked us into school with no money at all!

The next day, I showed up but no Scott. The day after that, no Scott, and the week after that, no Scott. Finally, they called me to the office to ask me about my friend Scott, and I was like, "ummm, we not really friends like that. I actually just met him and don't know him that well." I wasn't totally lying. I hadn't known him that long, but I did see him every day. Scott just wasn't ready for school at that time. He was known for years to work in a salon, and just when the word was out that the State Board of Cosmetology was in the area, he would get ghost and start working somewhere else, until they got hot on his trail again. He was like Leonardo DiCaprio in the movie *Catch Me If You Can*. He did this for years. Eventually, he went to one of the best schools for cosmetology. He still remains at the top of my list, as one of the most talented and gifted stylists I've ever known, and after 30 years or so, he is still in high demand and at the top of his game! This was indeed a friendship that made a major impact on my life.

  Beauty school was different for me. At that time, we had to wear all white every day. That in itself was pretty weird. In the beginning, I was doing pretty good in school. As I worked to get my first 300 hours, finger waves were a setback for sure. One day I became so frustrated trying to learn finger waving that I actually quit school! That's right, I quit. I cleaned out my locker, packed up my bags, and was on my way out the door. Just before I reached the exit, I noticed a class going on in the auditorium. As I slowed down to see what was going on, there stood this very charismatic, well dressed dude with major swag. It was the legendary hair stylist by the name of Barry Fletcher from the Maryland area. He had just won first prize at a recent Bronner Brothers hair competition in Atlanta, which was a Rolls Royce! He wore a custom-tailored zoot suit, and the women were giving him their full attention! As I left campus that day, the image of Barry stuck in my head. Up until that moment, I was questioning my decision about going to beauty school in the first place. Although I was partially going to school to become a better sales representative and to be a hair stylist, my general impression of men that did hair was that they were gay.

As a child, my grandmother owned a beauty salon, but I never wanted to go inside because I always felt like the guys in there were going to jump on me as soon as I walked in. I would later learn how foolish and homophobic I was, but at that time, I didn't know any better. However, witnessing Barry on stage, I could totally see myself on a stage educating one day.

During the next few days, I just sat around my apartment thinking about my next move. One afternoon, as I sat in my living room watching television, my mannequin was sitting on my coffee table and seemed to be looking right at me. Naturally, I started looking right back at her. Then, a conversation took place in my head. I had to ask myself if was truly going to let something like finger waves keep me from getting what I wanted? I got myself up off that sofa, grabbed my mannequin and wet her down, put some The Shampoo in her hair, and started to go to work. The Shampoo is a product that any person that ever stepped on the campus of DCU or attended any class or seminar with Dudley Products Inc. would never forget! By the end of that day, I had mastered finger waves!

Needless to say, I went back to school the very next day to show my instructor my work. My waves were so good, she didn't believe that I'd done them. She made me rinse them out and do them over in front of the entire class. At this point, I was so confident in my ability, I was thrilled to be in front of the class. In my mind, at that moment, I was Barry Fletcher on stage teaching my first class. After I showed my instructor, Ms. Poindexter, my skills, she gave me the name "Gold Finger," and from that day forward, things just came easy for me. Now that I had a vision of myself doing platform work like Barry, it gave me a clear and concise picture of where I was headed. I never thought all the time I'd spent honing my clipper skills would actually pay off, but now I seemed to be ahead of the game skill wise, and short hair quickly became my first area of expertise. Eventually, I even taught the Clippermetrics Advance class and even had a chance to revise the course curriculum based on my own technique of fading. You see, I simply needed to get past that one hurdle, and everything after that was golden. At the age of 23, besides graduating from high school, I hadn't yet completed anything, and I had to see this cosmetology school thing through to the end. I never saw myself as a quitter, but that's exactly what I would be if I didn't finish, as I hadn't finished college.

Every week at the graduation of the students who traveled from all over the world to take advance classes at the hair mecca, Dudley Products, a man named Marcus Eldridge would say this poem called "Don't Quit":

When things go wrong as they sometimes will,
When the road you're trudging seems all uphill
When funds are low and the debts are high,
And you want to smile, but you have to sigh,
When care is pressing you down a bit-
Rest if you must, but don't quit.

Life is strange with its twists and turns,
As every one of us sometimes learns,
And many a fellow turns about
When he might have won if he stuck it out.
Don't give up though the pace seems slow-
You may succeed with another blow.

Often the goal is nearer than
It seems to a fair and faltering man,
Often the struggler has given up
When he might have captured the victor's cup,
And he learned too late when the night came down,
How close he was to the golden crown.

Trust the Journey Embrace the Process

Success is failure turned inside out-
The silver tint of the clouds of doubt,
And you can never tell how close you are,
It may be near when it seems afar,
So stick to the fight when you're hardest hit, -
It's when thing seem worst that you mustn't quit.

Author Unknown

    It was amazing to me that all the years I ended up being a part of the Dudley Products company, Marcus would recite this poem with the same conviction every single week. I later learned that this poem also helped him get through many tough times in his life, and that's why he was so passionate every single time he recited it. Years later, I told him how much it helped me, to hear him every week, saying that poem. I can close my eyes at any given moment and see him as clear as day shouting, "NEVER GIVE UP, NEVER QUIT" in his pastor like manner, with tears in his eyes. He told me he was saying it for himself too, as a reminder, and that's why he said it with such passion. This was the beginning of me really starting to understand the power of programming the subconscious mind, by using positive affirmations, or pictures.

    One of the many good leadership qualities of Mr. Dudley was that he always gave his employees reading assignments. There were several books we were advised to read, but two of my favorites are *The 7 Habits of Highly Effective People* by Stephen R. Covey and *Think and Grow Rich*. The latter was originally written by Napoleon Hill, but I also read the other entitled *Think and Grow Rich, A Black Perspective* by Denis Kimbro. These books were extremely instrumental in my growth and future success. It also taught me the importance of consistently feeding your mind with books like these. I still get something from them every time I read them!

As I continued my schooling, more and more people sought me out to style their hair. As more people sought me out to style their hair, eventually, I thought to myself, I could be around women all day, get paid doing something fun, and flirt a little? Yeah, I told Mr. Dudley I was going to stay on this side of the business from this point on versus sales!

Once I decided to become an entrepreneur, not to mention a hair stylist, I shared this amazing career path with some of my close friends and family members. Initially, they thought I was crazy. My father thought I had totally lost my mind! He simply couldn't understand why I would quit college to "do hair." However, many people don't realize how noteworthy or diverse the role of the cosmetologist/barber can be. As I mentioned, I was first enticed by the thought of being around women all day, but it wasn't long before I realized the many things we do as cosmetologists that can sometimes positively affect generations to come. We become role models to the youth, and counselors to many others. Cosmetology is also one of the few professions licensed to touch the human body. It is important that we as professionals, maintain this standard of excellence in our industry.

Now that I had vision, I began to attract, as well as gravitate to others who were like minded and had true passion, artistry, skill, and an amazing level of intelligence as well as a burning desire to be successful. The friendships I created were friendships that all helped me become the person I am today. At the top of that list is a person I consider to be my brother, Alphonso McGriff III. Without going into any major detail, when he heard me speak once at an event and recognized I was amongst the conscious, he began to educate me to the politics that surrounded me that I was totally unaware. These are politics that exists in many aspects of the corporate world, and to thrive in that arena, you must learn the game. To this day, he is one of the most intelligent, strong, and unafraid men I know.

Another brother who is still one of the greatest stylists that I've ever had the pleasure to work with and befriend was Maurice Lemons. This was who everyone aspired to be like, or at least be on his level talent wise. He was from Oklahoma City. He had long hair that was unusual for a brother, drove a Delorean, like in the movie *Back to The Future* with the gull wing doors, and the license plate read, "SYATT." It took me a while to find out that it stood for See You At The Top. When you saw him get out of that car, you believed that if you made it to the top, you would certainly see Maurice Lemons right there too. As we had lunch one day, he asked me a question. He said to me," So are you in the industry to make a quick dollar, or are you in it for the love and the long haul?" It seemed as if I didn't answer this question in the right way, he wasn't going to be bothered with me any further. He had a strong background in the martial arts, so many times it was like talking to the famous martial artist Bruce Lee. Fortunately, my answer was good, as I replied," I'm in it for the love and the long haul." From that day, we began a great friendship, and he remained my greatest inspiration in the profession.

Soon I became a part of the National/International Dudley Styling team. I will never forget the first seminar I did was in Indiana during Christmas time. The theme of the seminar was "Holiday Up Do's." This was not my strongest area, but I was working with another veteran who was my lead person, so I felt ok. As all the sales reps were setting up for the show, I noticed a lot of whispering going on, then just before it was time to go on stage, Wilbert Artist, a sales rep, who I have been friends with to this day, told me I would be doing this seminar by myself because my lead person couldn't make it! WHAT! My first seminar, and they were going to just throw me out there. Well, once again, I learned a valuable lesson. I found out that even when you are not sure of yourself, if you carry yourself with confidence, and walk as if you absolutely belong where you are, people will respond to you accordingly, and that's just what I did. I remember saying to my first model as I released her not to let anyone touch her hair and walk gently because I was worried her up do would come tumbling down. I GOT THROUGH IT.

Later that year, I started feeling myself just a little, and found myself on stage with my two mentors, Maurice, and a young talent who later became like a sister to me, Brunetta Roberts. I thought I was doing something big time, and for me, I was. We were positioned in a triangular three point set up on stage, and I was in the front. I could hear both of them complementing my work as the audience focused and paid close attention to what I was doing. My up do was so tight, all I could think was I just might be on Maurice's level now. Five minutes after I was done, he was just finishing up his model, and his up do simply blew my stuff off the map! All I could think was *damn, I still have a long way to go*. Moments like this kept me humble and reminded me often that I always had things to learn. I learned I may be a big fish in my own pond, but there are always going to be bigger fish once you decide to get out there and really swim. For the next few years, all of us were who were a part of this team were looked at as celebrities when we did shows around the globe.

Working amongst the industries best helped me a lot. During this time, I did many things in Dudley Products. Outside of traveling, I worked in various areas of the advance department, which was led by the legendary Ms. Irene Parson. She was an old school stylist that could hang with the best of them. I believe there was nothing she couldn't do! Her electric energy kept everyone in such a positive place, and we all genuinely loved what we did so much. It was always said we didn't wear watches because we would stay all night until you got what you came to learn, and we did. Generally, we stayed teaching and supervising until about 1:00 am and sometimes even later

3

My First Salon Experience

I worked in the Dudley Salon that boasted thirty stylists, and once again, they were all super talented! When I first arrived, I mostly admired a stylist named Tabitha Gwynn. She was so humble but so good and was booked for an entire year in advance! In my book, as a new stylist with no clientele, that made her a living legend.

My first day in the salon was the most unforgettable experience ever. There were a lot of people hyping me up as this great stylist coming out of school to work in the salon, so when I arrived, everybody wanted to see just how good I was. They also gave me the station at the very front of the salon, where everyone in the waiting area could see me work. On this particular day, I had a client who wanted a roller set. It was the type of set that was called a snatch back, kind of like Helen and Mrs. Jefferson wore on the television show *The Jefferson's*. Well, because I was so fascinated with freeze curls when I was in school, I wasn't very well versed in roller setting. This was indeed my weakest area. Although humble, I still wanted to try my best to live up to the hype. I proceeded to set my client, then style her once she was dry. As I began to brush through her hair, trying to make it snatch back, it just wasn't working. This was due to me not understanding the importance of roller placement, so rather than over directing the rollers to get the desired look, I rolled them all on base, and the curls just sat on top of my client's head and would not cover her large forehead at all! This would be hard evidence demonstrating the importance of paying attention to every area of study during your education.

Back then, I used to wear custom tailored suits to work every day, due to the impact Barry Fletcher had on me. I worked so hard on that head and was so nervous that I literally sweat through my suit jacket! Finally, after everyone watched me struggle, my wonderful co-worker Lori Gwenn came to my rescue. The real insult to injury was that my next client had been watching me struggle the whole time. She wanted the same type of style that just made me sweat through my suit. She said to someone else but loud enough for me to hear," he's a nice guy and all, but he's not getting on my head today" as she walked out the door! On the inside, I was crushed. I left that day thinking to myself that one day that lady is going to be dying to get on my schedule. It is virtually impossible to find any person that is successful in any respect that has not failed many times before, and anyone who tells you different is simply not being honest with you. Remember, once you have failed at something, you are also one step closer to being successful at that very thing, as long as you don't give up. This failure would be one of many.

Building a clientele is something that truly deserves much more attention in cosmetology school than it gets. As a member of the Advisory Board of Cosmetology at Guilford Technical Community College here in North Carolina, I've strongly suggested we implement more attention to this area of the curriculum. It seemed to take forever to build a strong client base. It is especially challenging when you have bills along with family responsibilities as well. I did, however, have a little boost from my good friend Brunetta. One day I was sitting at home, sulking just a bit while watching *All My Children* because I didn't have any clients. Brunetta called me and asked why I wasn't at work? I told her that I didn't want to be sitting around all day doing nothing, while everyone else was busy. I told her it made me feel as though all the clients were thinking I must not be any good, since I didn't have any clients. Often, we think all the clients we had while in cosmetology school, will follow us to the salon once we graduate. This typically will not be the case. Bru, as I called her then gave me a dose of reality, like only she could. She said," If you don't bring yo ass to work" with her Alabama accent," you not ever gone have no damn clients!! You need to bring yo ass up here right now!" I honestly didn't like hearing what she said, but I knew she was right. From that day forward, I was in the salon all day, every day I was scheduled to be there. That's the beauty of making real friends that will tell you what you need to hear and not what they think you want to hear.

It wasn't long before I became very busy every day. While I was building my clientele, I took my time on every person that sat in my chair and gave them my best. Giving people quality treatment helped me build faster than any fancy business cards, though I did pass out cards everywhere I went. Today, the power of social media makes self-promotion much easier, and much more effective. I once saw someone drop one of my cards as they walked away, I had to develop tough skin to make it. I always believed one of the best ways to get back at people that made you feel less than was to become the most successful I could be and let that speak for me! Mr. Dudley often talked about how being rejected by women he was interested in, made him strive for success even more, and it worked for me as well!

For the next four years, I would travel all over the country doing seminars, working all the major trade shows like the *IBS* in New York, *Bronner Brothers* in Atlanta, *The*

Proud Lady in Chicago, the Bahamas and many other places around the country. I still worked in the salon, as well as in the advance department. Meanwhile, my girlfriend was also expecting my first born son, Scotty Bonds. Due to this, I really needed to step up my game. I'd heard all this talk about becoming a millionaire over the last five years, but it became increasingly more difficult to see how I was ever going to become one in this corporate structure. Finally, I decided to talk to Mr. Dudley about my future with the company. We sat in his big, white Cadillac, and I told him about the conversation I had with my mother about how much I loved being a part of Dudley Products. I also explained that I'd been working what seemed to be twenty hours a day in various capacities, but I needed to make more money. With a child on the way, I needed to know how I was going to become a millionaire? I asked if there was anything else I could do to make more money, and with no hesitation at all, he said "No." I sat there waiting in awkward silence expecting something to follow the "No," but there was nothing else said.

The following week, I turned in my resignation. Although I was truly hurt and very disappointed, due to the love I had for this company, I realized that potentially, Mr. Dudley saw something great in me and knew he had to set me free to fulfill my own destiny. I knew I would miss the many people who played such an important role in my development, but I also knew they all taught me things that prepared me for this next chapter in this journey.

4

A Whole New World Awaits Me

After having the conversation with Mr. Dudley in his car that day, I knew I had to come up with a plan. I remembered having a conversation with one of the advance students I taught, and she told me about the wonderful world of booth rent. I had been led to believe that booth rent was the worst thing that ever happened to the industry, but I now I had to explore this avenue. Upon graduating cosmetology school, it was highly recommended that new stylists work in a commission salon. This would help build both a clientele as well as more confidence in the craft of a stylist. Though there are pros and cons to both, as a booth renter, I was about to get a lot more than I was expecting. I had been out of school for about 4 years now, and had a pretty good clientele, working in the Dudley salon, but now I would be totally depending on my salon income.

I took my time deciding where I would start this new chapter in my career. I knew I wanted to be in a nice area and not in the hood. My choice in a potential location was not based on me thinking I was better. I had a particular type of clientele I wanted to attract and wanted them all to be comfortable where ever I was located. I believed that the clients who were comfortable in the more urban areas wouldn't have a problem coming to a nicer part of town, but those who might be considered more on the bougie side may not be willing to come to the more urban areas.

In my search for a salon to begin my new journey, I knew I had to continue to surround myself with talent and professionalism, so I visited several in the area. I would look to see what products the stylist used, how the salon was set up over all, and how the stylist carried themselves. The reputation of the salon was important to me. I knew it would always precede the perception of me, especially as a new stylist.

I can remember speaking with an owner at a salon I was considering. While talking to me, he was applying a relaxer. He only based around the hairline; He didn't wear any gloves, and he was applying the relaxer with her hands. Intuitively, this alone told me this was not the place for me. Although he was very successful and had a thriving salon, I knew I needed something else. Finally, someone told me about a salon called Boz & Company.

Morris Boswell, the owner of Boz & Company, was

a fairly eccentric type of guy. One of his most memorable outfits consisted of a construction hard hat, very fitted jeans, combat boots, and he often wore his prescription Ray Ban sun glasses that were super dark. However, this was one of the things that made people come to him. He simply was never afraid to be himself. He was a very successful stylist, college educated, and had good business sense. He was in the process of building a new salon right in the heart of downtown Greensboro, NC. I only heard good things about him, so I went to him to see what my instincts would tell me, and Bingo! He was the person, and Boz & Company was the place I'd been looking for!

The salon itself was beautiful, and Boz had the stylists that every salon should have. The original team included, Boz, Felicia, Robin, Peaches, Damion, Keith (RIP), Pam, and Crystal. I was different from everybody, but this was a good thing. We all were different and had our own select skills. I was the perfect addition, to the already perfect team.

My name was rapidly growing in the area, especially on the surrounding college campuses. My first week I made over $1500 in 1993! I remember asking Boz if it was always going to be like this? After all, I had been working day and night, just to make half of that over a two week period! He said, "as long as people keep coming to sit in your chair, it sure will be." I was so excited! However, several weeks later, school was let out for spring break, and all of my clients were gone; I was broke as hell! It was at that time I learned how to balance my clientele between working professionals and college students, and of course, those that didn't work at all. That was a horrible lesson, but it made me better and a smarter business person.

This salon experience at Boz & Co. would teach me, shape me, and prepare me for all that was to come. Back in the early 90's, people were different than they are now. Stylist were very different as well. There were no cell phones, tablets, Facebook, Instagram, etc. We actually talked to each other, but more importantly, we cared about each other, and we cared about the team. We worked long hours together, partied together, celebrated together, and typically had fun with each other every day. When there was a problem, we talked about it and moved on, and we didn't make it a priority to hurt one another outright or in a passive aggressive way. I can honestly say I genuinely loved everyone who was a part of the team.

Many of the most memorable and funny stories at Boz & Co. seemed to revolve around one of the stylist Debra, who went by Peaches. One of the best laughs, however, was not so much about her as it was about Boz. She and Boz had fallen out for some reason, so they weren't really speaking at the time. She was very well known for her hair replacement skills as well as her skill for waxing eye brows. Well, on this particular day, one of Boz's clients wanted to have her brows waxed, but she wasn't around, and since she and Boz weren't speaking, Boz didn't want to call her. So Boz told the client that he could do her brows for her. When I heard him volunteer, I immediately said in a joking way," Man, I didn't know you knew how to do brows" (since I'd never seen him do any waxing before). The client then looked at me to see if I was serious or just joking. I reassured her that if Boz said he could do them, then I was sure she would be fine. Boz proceeded to apply the wax, just as I'd seen Debra do in the past. He then placed the cloth on her brows and pressed it firmly in place, just as I'd seen Debra do as well. However, when he pulled the strip off, the inside of the brow that is supposed to be the thickest was really thin, and the outside of the brow, which is supposed to be the thinnest was really thick. It was like he moved the right brow to the left! I believe I laughed for the rest of that entire week! I couldn't get myself together. Now, I do believe that sometimes you have to *fake it, until you make it*, but this was definitely not one of those times. We all had one of the best laughs ever that day. Shortly thereafter, Boz and Debra reconciled their differences and things were right back on track. The salon team was truly like a family.

Boz and I became like best friends. He knew he could always count on me, and I knew I could count on him as well. When I decided to build my first home, Boz allowed me to charge my blue prints on his American Express card. Not to mention, that bill had to be paid at the end of the month, and they cost almost $1000. That showed me he believed in me and trusted me, and that meant a lot.

I always conducted myself the way I would want someone to conduct themselves in my salon I hoped to have one day. I always thought this would create good karma for me. I felt like it would be sowing good seeds for the future. Meanwhile, I was becoming one of the best short haircut stylists in the surrounding area. I always had a waiting list! Then, one day Boz hired a new stylist. Her name was Shonda Boyd.

Shonda was super slim, with a great big smile and personality to match. She was super talented. She worked upstairs at the salon and was a platform artist for a company called Joyce Williams. Her first day will forever be ingrained in my mind. When the first client she finished walked downstairs, her hair was flawless! It was a freeze curl type of style. Her hair was curled with such precision. It was incredible. Everybody immediately looked at me and said, "Uh oh Scott, what you gonna do?" I have to admit, I was absolutely shook on the inside, but I kept my calm on the outside. Later however, I walked outside and called my mentor Maurice, "Yo, it's this new girl at the salon, and she's got mad skill! I need to learn some new stuff!" He started laughing, but I was dead serious. He told me to be confident in what I know, and I'd be fine. He always said things that would require you to think very deeply, kind of like a kung fu master as I mentioned earlier, but that wasn't what I was looking to hear at that moment. Although I'd been around advance education the entire time I was at Dudley's, I was reminded once again just how important it was to continuously educate myself. I quickly learned that the moment that I think I know everything is the moment I would begin to decline. My problem wasn't that I thought I knew everything though. My problem was that I was always sharing all I had to give, but nobody was showing me much because they didn't think I needed it. I did

5

Beginning to Build My Dream

When I was 26, and my son Scotty was two years old, I began building my first home, and I remember being asked why I had to build a house like I was building for my first house? My response was that, for starters I could afford to, and it was what I wanted. In certain instances, you have to seize the moment or opportunity when it's there. Secondly, I said that this may be the only house I'll ever own, and if that was going to be the case, I wanted it to be to my liking. What they didn't know was that my real motivation was created much earlier in my life.

As a child, I lived in a small but nice two-bedroom apartment with my mother. My brother and sister were older than me, so they had already moved out. My father, who remains the most important man in my life, lived in the infamous Newark, New Jersey, also known as Brick City because Newark is not for the faint of heart, as you would often see tall all brick project housing in every direction, and you had to be hard to live there. Although my dad had a nice house, it was still surrounded by the hood. The street he lived on ran into Weequahic Avenue, where some of the most intimidating projects were located. Most of my close friends I grew up with lived in houses, but this one friend of mine lived in a spectacular home. Gary Lewis' father, Aubrey Lewis, did many great things, including having a very successful career in business working for the FW Woolworth Corporation now (Foot Locker Inc.) for thirty-seven years as the VP of corporate affairs. He was the most successful Black man most of us growing up in Montclair, NJ personally knew. Before we all had driver's licenses, we would have to catch rides to and from the parties we used to go to, and no matter who we were with, every time we dropped Gary off, people were amazed at his home. It was a huge, white house with a long walkway to the front door. It had a driveway that went all the way around to the back of the house. In addition, there was a guest house right next to the tennis court. From that early experience, I decided that I wanted my children to have that feeling I imagined Gary having every time someone saw his house. It was simply inspiring and left a life-long impression on me. I'm sure it motivated most of my friends to do well in life as well. I learned a valuable lesson from that experience, the *power of influence*.

While in my planning phase, I began by programming my subconscious mind. Everyplace in my apartment I had a picture of the house I was planning to build. My friends would visit and always ask why I had the picture everywhere? The picture was in front of my bed, so it would be the first and last thing I would see in the morning and at night. It was in front of the toilet, so when I sat down or stood up, I would have it on my mind, and it was on my front door, to remind me what I was going to work for everyday in the first place. Not many people outside of my inner circle knew any of this.

I credit my tunnel vision towards my goals to Anna Marie Hordsford, who played the role of Craig Jones' (Ice Cubes) mother (Mrs. Betty Jones) in the classic movie Friday, in addition to several other television and movie roles. I met her on a flight returning from California one Thanksgiving. The flight from California to North Carolina is pretty long, so naturally, I thought it would make sense to talk to the person sitting next to me. It's something about being around people, especially that close and not having any conversation that just doesn't feel right to me. Apparently, this young lady didn't feel the same way and had no interest in having any conversation with me. I finally got the memo and stopped trying to make conversation. After deciding to go to the restroom, as I got up, I saw Anna sitting right behind me but couldn't figure out why she looked so familiar to me. When I returned, I asked her "are you the lady from…" and before I could finish my sentence, she said, "Yes honey! Come sit next to me!" She told me that she saw how I was attempting to make conversation with the girl sitting next to me and noticed she didn't have much to say and said she would be glad to talk to me. She was one of the nicest people I've ever met.

During the conversation with Anna, I asked her what would she say helped her the most to become successful? She told me about programming the subconscious mind and told me she'd send me a few good books to read. One of the books was *Open Your Mind to Prosperity* by Catherine Ponder. It speaks about becoming successful, and I learned a tremendous amount. It was this book that I learned about what some call a vision board, but it was described as "the wheel of fortune.". Anna explained that this was one way to program your subconscious mind, and that it worked so well that it may even scare me. She told me not to be scared, to simply accept what I was blessed with, and keep it moving. Catherine Ponder explains it like this. You first start with a green card stock or construction paper. This represents wealth. In the center, you place a picture that represents your faith or spiritual belief. For example, if you are a Christian you might put a picture of a cross or maybe a Bible. If you are Muslim, you might put a star and crescent, Buddha if you are Buddhist, etc. Next, you find pictures that represent the things or goals you wish to accomplish. It was also important to place the things in the order you wanted them to occur. The last thing to do was focus on this board every day, every night, and any time in between. Anna was right, and it truly amazed me. "The wheel of fortune" worked, and it blew me away! My new upcoming home would definitely be placed on this board.

Saving money for this house required some sacrifices. One of my biggest was selling my BMW 535is. That was absolutely one of my most favorite cars. I instead, bought what I used to call my 1929 Honda hatchback. It was grey in color, but that was pretty much because it had no paint left on it. It would cut off on the highway sometimes, and I would coast to the shoulder and talk to it for a few. I would say," Come on now. I need you to hang in there for just a few more months;" then, I would say a little prayer, turn the key, and it would start right up! I remember sitting at a stop light one day and looking at these girls in the car next to me. At that very moment, I'd totally forgotten that I wasn't in my nice BMW, and I was driving this hooptie! The girls just started laughing and drove off. Secondly, I was homeless throughout the duration of the construction process. I couldn't afford to pay rent someplace and save enough money, so I temporarily moved in with my girlfriend. However, that was short lived. I was so focused on my goals that anything that didn't pertain to that goal became a distraction, and my relationship didn't survive.

Next, I stayed with my best friend Raymond O. Jones in Winston Salem and slept on his floor for a while.

Ray, as I call him, is another person that has inspired me immensely over the years. He would be considered second generational wealth. His father owned a few McDonald franchises for several years. Eventually, he sold them, and he and his dad were the first to introduce the salon suite concept in North Carolina. They opened two in Queen City of Charlotte, NC named Salon Central. He, as well as his dad, exemplify the greatest level of humility of anyone I've ever known. They are millionaires, but they would never openly tell anyone. I always jokingly say to him that he doesn't have to "pretend to be a regular dude." Now, let me be clear. He has paid his dues. His father didn't just hand everything over to him just because.

When we first met, he worked at the drive thru at one of their McDonald's, had a very humble apartment just around the corner from where I stayed, and was building on his future as well. The difference is that he didn't have to start from zero, and he had the guidance of his father. I will always remember his father saying to me that I was a diamond in the rough, that I just needed to stay the course, and I would be alright. That meant a lot to me coming from such an incredible man. Next, while my son's mother was out of town on business for a month, she allowed me to stay at her house so I could take care of our son. I have to admit that although we were not together at that point, she was extremely helpful and instrumental in my early success. I will always remember her buying my first custom tailored suit. She was a person that always believed in me, and people like that really help you believe in yourself even more!

Eventually, I decided to take a friend up on his offer to stay at his house because as he told me, he was never there. Because of his openly gay lifestyle, I was somewhat apprehensive about living with him. I didn't want anyone getting the wrong idea about me. With no other options, I decided to take him up on his offer. He told me where he kept the spare key, so I decided to check it out. I felt like it would be cool for a while, so I set up the little guest room. I even went out and bought groceries and organized them in the kitchen. Abruptly, about a week later after working all day long, the salon phone rings, and my new roommate proceeded to tell me how he had some company coming in from Atlanta, and "I had to come get all my shit." I couldn't believe this was happening. Not only was it the end of a 12 or 13 hour day in the salon, and about 9:30 pm in the evening, but I literally had no place to go. I went to his house, got "my shit," put everything in my 1929 Honda hatchback, and just sat there trying to figure out where I would possibly go next. I finally ended up at another friend's house named Mike Mathews.

The irony was that Mike was responsible for me finding the property I was building my house on in the first place. For the next four months, I slept on his fairly torn, vinyl love seat in the living room. And while all of this was going on, there were many nights that after working all day, I would go out to my house and do much of the work myself using the temporary power source, moving a single spot light from room to room. I did not have time to become stagnant or complacent.

It took about nine months to complete construction, but I finally finished! After growing up in an apartment all of my life, this felt like a huge accomplishment. To demonstrate that he recognized my hard work, Boz gifted me with a very nice house warming party, as one of my dreams had finally come true. Conquering this made me believe that I could truly do anything. However, there was just one more thing I needed to do to feel really good. I had to get me a new whip! My friend, Mike, who let me sleep on his sofa during the last four months of construction, worked at the Acura dealership. He knew I wanted a Legend Coupe, so he called me one night while I was at work and told me to sell my 1929 Honda hatchback because he had two cars for me to choose between, so I sold my car for $500.

Boz drove me to the dealership, and when we pulled up, there sat a pearl white Acura Legend Coupe! The other was nice, but I knew which one I wanted as soon as I saw it. Mike loaned me $1500 to add to the $500 I already had, and off I went! He never told me he was planning to do that. What he did say was that he would make sure I drove off with a new car that night, and he was right. I knew this was good karma from all my hard work. Now that things had come full circle. All the sacrifices I'd made at the beginning of this journey had all paid off. Life was good :-)

6

On to The Next Thing! (The Right Angle)

My time at Boz & Co. continued to be phenomenal, but one day someone told me about a salon that was for sale. Because it was in one of the best parts of town, I wasn't really thinking I would be able to afford it, but I remembered hearing Mr. Dudley say how he was going to build this event center on the Dudley Cosmetology University campus, and he had no idea where the money would come from. He was going to simply, trust God. He simply believed he could do it, and he did. I truly believed that if God intended for me to have it, then I would.

Though the salon and equipment were pretty nice, the biggest problem for the most part was the horrible, dark green carpet on the entire floor. However, all in all, I saw the potential. I was told that the present owner was a drug dealer but not a hair stylist, and he paid a large amount to the previous owner. For this reason, he was trying to get a good return on his investment, but there was one problem. He didn't own anything to sell. The space was being leased, and so was the equipment.

I first called the company that was leasing the equipment. I then found out that the lease was in default, and there hadn't been a payment in five months. The building lease was also behind, and it was near its end. I decided to move forward on this. I had to let the guy who was selling the salon know that unfortunately, he didn't have anything for me to buy. I believe he knew that from the start; he just didn't know I would find out. Next, I needed to talk to the company leasing the equipment to see if I could negotiate a price to keep it. I wasn't sure how much I should offer, so I sought council from my good friend, Parker Washburn, who is the daughter of the late Mrs. Leon and owner of the Leon's Beauty School and salon chain. When I asked her how much I should offer for the equipment, the price she gave me was so low. I was embarrassed to even repeat it! I didn't want the people to be insulted. Parker went on to teach me about depreciation and how it applies to the salon equipment. Because salon equipment depreciates a tremendous amount, she explained to never pay top dollar for used equipment. This was the first of many things she would teach me over the years.

The amount I offered was still about $200-$300 more than Parker suggested. I just couldn't imagine them accepting the number she'd given me. Though I didn't know it then, I eventually learned how people who have money never pay regular price, but common people, always pay top dollar. Unfortunately, the leasing company turned down my offer, so I told them to come get it. At that point, I began planning. I had no idea how I was going to do this, and even more, I didn't know where I would get stylist to work there.

  I also had to figure out how to tell Boz I was going to be leaving soon. This was very difficult. We were so cool, and I enjoyed his salon, but it was time to go to the next level. Unfortunately, things sometimes can go awry when a stylist leaves a salon they've worked in for some time. Though I can't really say it turned bad, it was very awkward. You could feel the tension in the air. One of the many things Boz said that always remained in the back of my mind was this. He said that the stress that comes with owning a booth rent salon is almost not worth the little bit of profit you make as the owner. In due time, this proved to be a profound statement, but this was something I had to learn on my own.

  For the next month or so, I would work long days at Boz & Co, and then leave there and go to work on my new salon remodel. Outside of my home, this was my second biggest project. I needed to put something together that would be appealing to many others. I wanted to be different. At that time, it seemed that White owned salons were always very well put together, and nice, Black owned salons seemed scarce. I wanted to set a standard for Black salon ownership.

    I continued to strive towards my goal of becoming a salon owner. During this time, I was also working for L'Oréal, representing many different product lines under the Cosmair umbrella including the well known brand of Mizani, and still doing shows around the country. Maurice, still my mentor at that time, was now the Artistic Director there. He pulled all of the best people together to be a part of that team. He used to always tell me to "stay ready" because when the opportunity came about, you had to show up. Being a part of this team, created many great opportunities. I really began to understand the power of networking during this time, as I met many stylists from around the globe. I also met people who help my salon endeavors become a reality. While working at the Bronner Brothers Show in Atlanta, GA. I met the owner of Buy-Rite Beauty Supply. After taking some time speaking with him, he helped me find financing for all of the equipment I needed. Buy-Rite would assist me with my future salons as well. I learned that although purchasing things using cash can be good, financing or leasing big ticket items can be beneficial from a tax standpoint because depreciation can be written off annually. I also learned that having a good relationship with a trusted accountant or CPA is definitely key for anyone in business. Financially, they can help determine the best route to pursue.

    After countless late night hours working what

seemed to have been 24 hours a day, I finally was at the point that I was ready to open my salon. It took me just a little over a month but turned out to be a very beautiful place. I re-did the floors and made them look like marble. I repainted all the trim a rust color and repainted the walls white. I designed the mirrors for the stations, had them custom cut and mounted them myself. I even found this vintage plant vine made of metal, and I cut a branch for each station, painted it, and placed it at the corner of every mirror. I had a beautiful, wood tone ceiling fan that matched my stations with lights that were controlled with a dimmer switch that really made the atmosphere sexy, especially during the evening hours! The final touch was the large, palm tree plants that were throughout the salon. I decided to call it The Right Angle. The funny thing is other than when I first decided to open a salon, I never thought about how I would get stylist to work there. I just *trusted the process*, and every night I was in there working until the crack of dawn, *I saw the vision* of the stations being filled and *flooded my subconscious mind with the end resul*t.

    To keep the pressure on me, my new girlfriend, a gifted nail technician, was pregnant with my second son who would be named Kamari Rashad Bonds. Scotty, my first son was now six years old. I never imagined having two children with two different women. I had no choice but to grind. It was a must that I take care of my kids.

    What happened next was amazing! The first week I was open, this beautiful, young woman came to work with me named Tiffany Goins (RIP). She was eager to learn; she was intelligent; she was a spiritual person and very pleasant. It wasn't long after Tiffany that I had a full team, and just like my other salon experiences, I had all of the personalities you'd expect to have. The team included Keith Davis whom I previously worked with at Boz & Co. I never did anything underhanded to get him to join me. We just became such great friends, work simply wouldn't be the same without him. He accepted me just as I was, and I did the same for him. Although he was openly gay, he was always around lots of females, and enjoyed keeping me up to date about how they felt about me! He was like a brother to me, and we always looked out for one another. He was one of the first people I was able to give $500 and tell them not to worry about paying me back. I just wanted to help him get back on his feet at that time. He always seemed to be in some type of struggle, but that was just who he was, and everybody still loved him. He never owned a car the entire time we were friends but always had one of his clients bring him to work, or he would catch a cab. I didn't realize it at that time, but these were seeds I was sowing, and I had no idea of the blessings that would eventually find me at the right time.

    Then, there was Wanda Graves. She was my son Scotty's great aunt. She was a very different type of person to put it mildly, but if you ever really took the time to get to know her, you would see all kinds of good and beautiful things in her. She would seemingly just fall in the salon, like she was in a wind storm or something, and if you watched her work, you would be totally lost in trying to figure out what she was about to create, but once she was finished, it would always be a beautiful work of art! Once while she was working on a client, I came over to talk to her, and I asked if she and her client were related because I thought they favored one another. Well, little did I know, that was the wrong thing to say to her. When she was finished, she asked me to come to the back of the salon and went off on me. She was insulted by my question because she thought her client was not that attractive and did not like me saying they favored. This is when I started to realize that being a salon owner, you had to learn how to deal with different personalities. For example, you wouldn't deal with LeBron James the same way you would deal with a rookie, and the same would prove to be true in dealing with various personalities in the salon.

Next there was Paula who was also a young stylist. She was a sweet heart as well, but boy did she stretch the truth! I can remember her telling me her mother was an air plane pilot for Delta Air. When she told me this, I thought that I would've heard about such a person, considering to my knowledge at least, there were no Black female pilots at that time. When I finally met her mother in person, I was so excited to talk to her to hear more about how she became a pilot and all. When I said to her, "So Paula tells me you're a pilot for Delta," she said, "Boy, I ain't no pilot. I'm a flight attendant!" The real shock was Paula was standing right there while we were talking, as if her mother was going to go along with what she had told me. She also told me that her father was going to buy her a new BMW, and when it was all said and done, he got her a VW! Not that there is anything wrong with a VW, as I have had a few myself, but it's certainly for far cry from a BMW! It kind of became the salon joke that Paula always stretched the truth a little, but it was all in fun.

There was also my great friend LaChetta Wright. We worked together at Dudley Products, and she was not only a stylist but also held a chemistry degree from NC A&T State University and worked in the laboratory in product development at Dudley Products. She was very attractive, intelligent, and driven, but kind of stayed to herself on many levels. She always spoke so highly of me, and although it made me feel good, it made me always try to live up to all the wonderful things she had to say.

The others were the nail tech, whose name was Tiffany, and she was phenomenal at her craft as well. George Morgan was an older gentleman who was a weave specialist and seemed to never leave the salon. I would leave work, and he would be there, and when I returned in the morning, he would be there! I really wasn't sure if he ever left the salon, but what I was sure of was that I could trust him. I would never bring someone aboard I felt that I couldn't trust. Then, there was Nikki who was the first young stylist I personally took under my wings and helped her grow in the salon. She absorbed everything and is still thriving in the business. Lastly, there was Felicia who was a seasoned stylist as well that had recently moved back to Greensboro from Atlanta. In less than three months, we were a team of nine stylists, and two nail technicians. This was more than I could've ever hoped for. Life seemed to be as good as it could get!

  I made it top priority to show these people that I genuinely cared about them. I was always anxious to share whatever I could with my team. If I knew how to do something that someone else wanted to learn, I would work with that person until he/she got it. That was the mentality that was instilled in me as an educator at Dudley Products. It is my belief that when having knowledge about certain things, it becomes my responsibility to share. By sharing, we open ourselves up to receive more. This is something that takes many people years to learn. It's the same principle as tithing. Whenever we had our salon meetings, I would always share things to motivate and encourage them. I would tell them about books that I learned about during my time at Dudley Products. I would create incentives for them to stay motivated. I would have fantastic parties at my home and invite everyone. I always stayed humble and never boasted about anything. I welcomed the people I worked with to be a part of my circle of friends, despite being advised not to. For me, this style of leading was a necessity for harmony amongst everyone.

During this time, I realized how important it is to get to know the individual as well as build the team. Teams usually have super stars, and super stars have to be dealt with very carefully. You must always allow them to shine but maintain your position as the leader of your team. I would say to my team, from time to time "This salon is my dream, and its beautiful to be able to choose the people you want to be a part of your dream." Some stylists might need to feel needed, and some just want to come to work, get their work done, and go about their business. There are also the ones who are simply hungry and willing to go get it! Morgan was at the top of that list. I used to call people like this piranhas! Morgan, in addition to, Paula would take absolutely anybody that walked through that door, and if a client wanted something that they were not sure how to do, they'd figure it out! I called them the piranha squad!

The pinnacle of this salon was when we decided to run a television commercial. I'm not sure where the idea derived, but it would prove to be a good one. Typically, those who own booth rent salons don't spend on advertising for the entire salon because booth rent income would remain the same either way. At this point of my career, I didn't need any more clients because I was already super busy. However, I always said I wanted everyone around me to be successful. *I think the success of the people you work with should be equally as important as your own.* With this in mind, I offered to pay half of the cost of the commercial spot and allowed my team to split the other half amongst themselves. Not only did we have overwhelming success, but it showed my team that I was willing to put my money where my mouth was. We ran the commercial on BET, and we were also the first Black salon to do such advertising in the area. The result was having days that were standing room only. Everyone was busy and making money!

Shortly after this success, I had the opportunity to do a live interview on the local Fox news station along with another well known stylist from the nearby area. When I'm in those types of situations, I'm typically extremely nervous on the inside at least. On the outside, I am told I appear calm. This was also the case whenever I was on stage as a platform artist. It was amazing being on live television, and that too gave the salon a tremendous boost. Things were great! I would often sit in my car after work and look inside the salon from the windows facing the street, talk to God, and simply say how grateful I was.

Now that things were going so well, it was time to use my blessing to benefit others. For as long as I can remember, I've always had a great love for our youth. I started a scholarship with the profit from selling snacks in the salon along with my own contribution, for young African American boys at James B. Dudley High School in Greensboro, NC called the Black Diamond Award. I was inspired to do this as I was invited to be a part of their career day for males only for a couple of years. The administrator in charge would frequently ask me what I was saying to these kids, as they all only wanted to stay at my booth and continue to listen to what I had to say. Although I'm pretty salt and pepper in my look and my age is becoming less of a mystery, I can still take myself right back to their age once I begin to speak with them. I try to make myself as relatable as possible, and never do I want to come off as being judgmental. What I realized the most with this group of young Black men was that they simply wanted to feel like someone genuinely cared about them. The reality is that I understood that there is a large majority of these young men who are one bad experience from being ruined for a long time. Subsequently, I also knew that there are also a large majority who are one experience from being extraordinary! I wanted to help in any way I could. Because many of these young men lacked a male role model, they seemed to desire a bond with a male who cared.

As an entrepreneur, I believe it is my responsibility to use my success, position of influence, and whatever other blessings I may have to help our youth be everything they have the potential to be in life. These youths will become our care takers and leaders of tomorrow.

7

The Change to Come

As my three-year lease approached its end, I saw a shift begin. This became more evident when I decided to purchase my first brand new car! While at the bank one day, I sat down with a personal banker who explained to me how I could use an equity line of credit. Because I used a lot of my own money to build my house, I had a $22,000 line of credit, due to the equity I'd established. It was at this point I should have invested in some other properties as I mentioned earlier, or at least into some type of appreciating assets. However, I didn't have any real guidance, so I ended up purchasing a new car! I didn't use my entire line of credit for this, but it allowed me to have the necessary down payment. It was the new '98 Lexus GS400, and I was one of the first to have one. This was a time I'll never forget. Everywhere I went, heads would turn, as nobody had really seen this new body style. I felt like I was on top of the world! These are things that are important to many of us when we are young. Over time as one matures, you will learn about things far more valuable, and worthy of investing in.

I soon learned that with new things comes jealousy. What bothered me most is that I've always taken delight in other's success, so I wanted everyone to be successful in my business. I've always wanted the people around me to be able to have whatever made them feel successful. I realized that many people talk about their dreams but put no real action behind their words. Those are typically the people that become "fans" or simply envious of others.

Also, during this time, I got into a serious relationship with a woman who would eventually become my first wife. Nobody had ever seen me so serious about anyone. It seemed as if my new relationship changed the energy in my salon, and I didn't like it. I decided to make a move for the better. I decided to upgrade my salon. I wanted to build something much greater. My initial plan was to ask my old friend Boz if he would like to partner up in this venture. We'd since reconciled our friendship. When I shared this with my now fiancé, she suggested that I let her be my partner instead. As much as this idea sounded good, I was always a bit hesitant to have a business with my spouse because I'd heard so many horror stories about couples that end in divorce. Typically, it's the man that loses everything, and although I was very much in love, I still had to be smart enough to at least consider all the possibilities here. Mr. Jones, my friend Ray's father who told me I was a diamond in the rough, also told me several years ago, to always try to avoid partnerships when possible, as more often than not, they end bad. I chose to ignore this advice. I instead followed love, and I decided to partner up with my fiancé'. She was the granddaughter and daughter of very successful attorneys, although her father passed away before we met. Her grandfather gave us $50,000 as a wedding gift that we planned to use to build a new house. There was never any intention to use any of that money for the new salon, but we eventually used about $8000.

  After searching, we found a location for the new salon that was brand new and started the process of making this dream a reality. Although I'd redone my first salon all by myself, this project was going to take a lot more. In the commercial retail world, they have what is known as a vanilla box. This is a space that is literally a big, rectangular space with four walls and nothing else. It is up to you to come up with your floor plan design and make it happen. This was somewhat intimidating as it was essentially like building my second home. This was a very big challenge. I was about to learn how to do things I had no idea I could do, but after having great success with my first venture, I believed I could tackle anything.

8

Lessons Learned

During the construction of Scott Bonds Salon, I learned many lessons that certainly had a tremendous affect on me. In hindsight, I should've kept the name of my salons the same from the beginning. It was my fiancé's idea to name this salon after myself because I had such a great reputation and was very well known. Admittedly, I did like the way it sounded, but I wasn't thinking about the branding aspect. Changing the name each time I opened a new salon wasn't the best idea. There were many other lessons that were good, but many were very painful.

In the beginning, it was familiar and felt fantastic. I was still working at my other salon, The Right Angle, while doing construction again literally all night. My lease agreement included sheet rocking four interior walls, but any additional walls was my responsibility. Because the ceilings were very high, there were steel support beams just above the drop ceiling, and the walls that my stations were to be placed had to be secured to them. It was also my first time working with metal studs, instead of wooden 2x4's, so there were some things I had to learn once again. I learned how to do most of these things by reading Home Depot books. The most important part of doing most things was having the right tools. I also remember reading Henry Ford saying he didn't need to know everything. He just needed the people around him to know the things he didn't. My friend Mike whose sofa I'd previously slept on during the latter part of the construction of my house, had become one of those people who knew everything I didn't know about construction, and helped tremendously during this time. We used to do many home improvement jobs together and he could do just about anything. Mike had an engineering degree from NC A&T State University. Unfortunately, he was my example of someone who could be very financially secure if he simply handled his business. His biggest problem was his heart was just too big. He tried to take on every job that was available and often would spread himself too thin. It really had nothing to do with him trying to make a lot of money, but he could never tell anyone "no." When things got too hectic for him, he would simply not show up and leave the job incomplete.

    After about two months, things began really taking shape. We had a brand new computer system that had the latest salon software for inventory as well as scheduling, mahogany wood floors, beautiful black and wood tone styling stations with matching shampoo stations and front desk. The mirrors extended from the top of the stations, 16 feet up to the high ceilings, track lights brightened all the eight stations, and we had more than enough dryers that included ottomans for clients to rest their feet while under the dryer. After we painted the entire salon and saw everything put together, I told my fiancé that the color we chose didn't create the right feeling for the salon, and the very next day, we completely repainted. We topped it all off with a complimentary gourmet coffee bar as well as providing soft drinks and wine. I tried to cover all the needs of both stylists and clients. The most expensive item was the exterior sign on the building. It was a lighted sign that cost $5000! This was something I should have paid closer attention to in my lease agreement. It could have been the one thing that may have swayed my decision to open in this location. At the time though, I didn't pay attention to the fine print on the lease that stated everyone had to have the same type of signage.

    The biggest difference with this salon though would be that this was going to be a commission salon. I lost most of my stylists when I made this change. Rarely will a booth renter switch to commission. If so, it's usually because the stylist has had some bad tax problems and trying to start over. Being responsible to pay taxes can be one of the most challenging things for a stylist that chooses to rent a booth.

To ask someone to take a good percentage of hard earned money on a quarterly basis and send it to some invisible entity that somehow has a lot of power, is hard, but the sooner this habit is formed the better.

In most cases, when starting a commission salon, this option will likely attract stylists that have recently graduated from cosmetology school. In other instances, this avenue may attract a few seasoned stylists that are simply looking for change. Whatever direction chosen, there will be challenges. Booth renters who are seasoned, sometimes come with bad habits, and at times are only concerned with themselves. Because working in a booth rent salon without a clientele can be stressful, it is also advised that new stylist coming out of school begin working in a commission salon as mentioned previously. Furthermore, new stylist benefit greatly when they are around experienced stylists in a structured work environment, with plenty of advanced education. They are also less likely to pick up bad habits as well.

I was fortunate to have a couple of stylists come with me from The Right Angle that tried to switch to being on commission, but that didn't last long. My close friend Keith Davis (RIP) was my rock at this point. Eventually, I had to hire all new stylists. Every member of my new team besides Keith, were recent graduates, which meant I had a lot of work ahead of me. During this experience, I was about to get a master's degree in entrepreneurship.

At the top of my list of things to do was to keep my young team motivated. I also had to train each of them on all I could. Although they were all very ambitious, I spent a good amount of time fixing dissatisfied clients. Teishma Brown was at the top of this ambitious group. She had no fear of anything. She filled the place that Tiffany and Nikki from The Right Angle once occupied as my salon little sister. There was also a new Tiffany and a young lady named Odessa who helped to keep the salon flowing. Once I began having educational training regularly, things began to get a little better. I also started to attract a few more stylists interested in joining the new team. Unfortunately, I still wasn't getting the people I desired. One stylist was a little older, probably in her late 30's to early 40's. She was kind of rough around the edges. Not only did she come with a lot of bad habits. She thought she knew everything yet destroyed the hair of most of the clients that sat in her chair. Though she was a fairly-skilled barber, she wasn't a good fit. There was also a young stylist that was pretty good, but she just couldn't seem to stop making babies! My fiancé and I did everything imaginable to help her including getting her a part time job while she worked on building a clientele and giving her furniture for her children's bedroom. In the end, she proved to be disloyal. I was furious. I thought helping her would show her how much we genuinely cared and create some loyalty as well. Once I realized that was not the case, I began to understand that when you do things for people, you should never do them expecting something in return. I seemed to have had a string of people that just didn't fit. I even had a nail technician move all of her things in the middle of the night, after only being there for a week!

I had to start being a bit more selective about who I decided to bring in as new stylists. Once again, I needed to get all of my stations filled, and found myself rushing *the process*. After several months, the new team began to take shape. Most of them were younger stylists, and I knew they could become very discouraged in the blink of an eye. I was still hopeful that I would be able to have a diverse team, and it wasn't long before I was able to get two new stylists that helped improve things. Bill Pettiford was an older gentleman and somewhat of a Greensboro legend. He came to my salon with a desire to learn more than he knew and to help however he could. Many times, he was my assistant, and he was known for his legendary shampoo that made women's toes curl. Kristen Hovey played a special role because she could do things with color that most of the team did not know how to do. This was typical with White stylists. It was 2001, and from what I'd experienced, White stylists seemed to know cutting and color really well, and Black stylists did more relaxers and some color services well (on average). Though Black stylist can make a lot of money, working with White stylists revealed how much more money is made on the other side. The crazy thing to me is that it usually takes a lot more time to provide the services we provide to Black clients than what we provide to White clients, but we made so much less back then. I worked with a guy who shared the same work ethic as myself once at another salon, but he made about $1000-$1500 a day! That was a real eye opener. This is why I highly recommend Black stylists to get as much color education as they possibly can in school, as well as taking advance color classes upon graduating. This in addition to services that all people can benefit from, such as hair replacement techniques, can close the earning disparity greatly. I'm happy to say that gap has changed significantly in 2019.

One of the biggest challenges having Kristen there was that the other stylists would sometimes be in the salon all day and may have made $100-$150. Kristen would come in and work about three hours and would make $300 or more. That didn't always make the rest of the team feel so great. It was good for the salon though, considering we were trying to build on the commission model.

 Attempting this new system was especially challenging also because we had ADP Payroll Services doing our payroll, which included FICA taxes, social security, unemployment taxes, and what appeared to be every tax imaginable. It felt like I was paying sales and use tax every other day. I seemed to be going under water faster by the second. However, I was still determined to make this this work. One day while riding around with my fiancé, we looked at some new cars, and I remember test driving a new

Corvette. Later that day as we pulled up to the salon, we were talking about making enough money so that we could buy things we really wanted and not have to think so hard about the financial impact, and at the same time, we both said "and this salon is not the answer!" We both laughed at the same time but also knew there was some truth to the statement.

I decided to run another television ad, as I remembered the success we had at The Right Angle. The commercial looked fantastic, but because I chose to run it on the Lifetime channel instead of BET as I did before, it didn't go as well this time. That same year in September, I got married, and upon my return from the honeymoon, a few stylists decided to leave, one of which was Kristen. I couldn't be upset with her, as I didn't know enough about the things she needed most to be taught to her that would allow her to reach her full potential. The good thing was she went about leaving professionally and gave me a two-week notice. Because of that, and the bond we formed, we are still great friends to this day. She now has her own thriving salon, and I couldn't be more proud of her.

Eventually, I would have to make the decision to go back to being a booth rent salon for the sake of saving my business. I had to try to survive by getting good, professional stylist willing to pay what some considered to be high rent. Once again, the disparity between what White salons charge and what Black salons charge is also a world apart. I was now learning another valuable lesson. Sometimes when things are going very well in your business, we can get too excited and desire to expand, but this often can bring about challenges that may cause your demise.

One day I had a stylist stop by to inquire about working with us. This was another White stylist. He went on to tell me that there were six stylists in all looking for a place to work. The reason was, the owner of the salon they all presently worked at had recently decided to expand and leased the space next door. This caused her rent to increase to $5000 a month! Suddenly, things began to change, and she couldn't afford to stay there and was now closing. Although this was unfortunate for her, it was a tremendous opportunity for us. We met with everyone one evening, and I put together the best offer ever for them. The salon they were leaving was charging about $200 a week. I offered them a rate of $165 a week! Unfortunately, none of them decide to work at the salon. Later, I found out that it was because they were uncomfortable about it being a Black owned salon, and they were concerned about how their clients would react.

I would soon acquire another stylist by the name of Harold Berry who was like a great breath of fresh air. Typically, when you have two, straight male stylists in the same space, they are bound to become good friends. It's almost like a fraternity within a fraternity. Harold was very involved in his church, and we often had great conversations about religion and spirituality in general, but at the end of the day, he was a great guy with a big heart. Once as we were having a salon meeting, he recognized the hard time I was going through and compared this time in my life to the biblical story of Job. As he spoke, tears filled his eyes. He seemed to be able to feel the weight that was upon me at the time, and almost everyone else's tears were to follow. The last member of this ever evolving team was David. David was an openly gay stylist, whose life seem to be one big party! He worked hard and partied even harder. He always had a crazy story to tell you about what happened the night before. As crazy as he was, he was still always very encouraging, unless of course he was mad about something. Once we had a salon meeting, and he was mad at me for some reason, so while the rest of the team met. David, who lived just across the street from the salon, decided not to attend, but still stand in his front yard where he could clearly be seen, to demonstrate his defiance. Looking back, it really was pretty hilarious. We were now in the second year of being open, and although my salon wasn't making me rich by any means, I did create a few friends that would help me through the hard times ahead.

  Though my chairs were never filled completely, my team, along with the money I was making was enough to sustain the salon. Most booth rent salon owners work just as hard as their renters. I had become a slave to my own business. I was slowly beginning to regret every decision I'd made to open this new salon. I sold my Lexus and downgraded to a Honda Rodeo that I convinced myself kind of looked like a BMW X5, and I also trimmed my spending habits tremendously. With all this, I was still struggling. I literally had poured my heart and soul into this venture and was losing! Most of all, my marriage took several turns for the worst, and I was now learning how difficult it could be to keep yourself together when you come to work and to leave the personal stuff home. Unfortunately, I also learned that I wasn't so good at doing that.

In the beginning, my wife was a big part of the everyday functioning of the business. Having her there was a pretty good thing, but when things went bad, her not being there made things even worse. During this time, I was so unhappy and sad that I became a person I didn't even recognize and was very unpleasant to be around for everybody. I lost many clients during this tough time, but I really didn't even care. All I knew was that my marriage was getting worse and worse, and I had to figure things out. I lost so much weight due to my stress; my fingers even lost weight to the point my wedding band wouldn't even stay on my finger. I had become an emotional and physical wreck. I was so heartbroken that there were many days I would be at the gym working out, and tears would be streaming down my cheeks as I tried to make it seem as if I were just sweating a lot. This was a huge lesson in managing my emotions when dealing with personal life storms and business.

As things continued to get worse on all levels, I simply wanted to make it to the end of my lease and close the doors. I attempted to sell the business and even got as close as drawing up a contract for $30,000 with someone. Upon telling the owner of the building I was going to sell the business, I wanted to know if the lease amount would remain the same for the new owner. They informed me that they knew I was struggling, and they already had someone planning to take over my space when my lease was up. As you could imagine, I was crushed. There seemed to be nothing good happening for me at all. I would eventually sell all of my equipment and close the doors. To add insult to injury, a couple of weeks later, as I drove past what was my salon, I saw the beautiful mahogany floors and my tall mirrors smashed and stuffed in the dumpster.

9

Down... But Not Out.

After closing Scott Bonds Salon, I found myself back on the same street I began my salon ownership with The Right Angle. Back then, this salon was owned by a good friend of mine, Sheila Parquet (RIP), and it was called Panache. She expanded around the same time I did but on a much grander level. She had investors and all as she built a multi-million-dollar salon named Chakras by Panache right in the heart of the downtown area. Anyway, this salon had been taken over by someone else. It was now named Robi's, and it was still very nice just as I remembered. When I decided to work there, I decided to bring my friend Harold Berry with me. Harold was always such a positive force in my world, and it was good to continue having him around.

As I began to recover from all I'd been through from a business standpoint, I continued trying to save my marriage but to no avail. Eventually, my wife and I would separate for the last time before we divorced. I took the time to work on my craft and repair the financial damage I'd suffered over the past three and a half years. I decided I wanted to learn more about doing White clients, and Sheila from Chakras had been trying to get me to work with her for several years now, so it made sense to join her team. I tried to work out a part-time booth rent rate where I was, but they were not interested. Fortunate for me, Sheila had a friend, Lori Carter, who owned a booth rent salon, Salon Envy, which was just around the corner from Chakras downtown. My clients were a little shocked because this place was nothing like the other places I'd worked, but for me, it was the change I needed. I decided to work at Salon Envy and split my week working with Sheila at Chakras. This experience was very different and somewhat challenging.

  Once again, just as when I first started at the Dudley Salon, Sheila hyped me up. Apparently, she was under the impression that I was very experienced with all hair types, but that was simply not the case. As I mentioned earlier, as a Black stylist, I was good at what I was good at. I could relax almost anyone, and they not experience any irritation. I could also cut with the best of them, but what I knew about color was not even close to what these talented stylists knew. She even had me listed as a master stylist which was major. Moments like this you can embrace and adjust to, but when people are spending almost $200 for a cut and some high lights, you need to be able to deliver. I simply went there to learn and never asked for all I got.

There was an older woman who ran the front desk, and she volunteered herself to me to practice. Somehow, I managed to do a really good job round brushing her hair, despite never doing it before. She asked a lot of personal questions concerning my marital status, as I later found out she was interested in me. However, she wasn't too helpful once she realized I had no interest in her though. I was really clueless about how things worked in this type of environment.

I remember the first client I had on my schedule during my first real day on the floor was getting a haircut and blow dry. I thought that the clients only wore smocks because I didn't see any capes around, so I proceeded. As I was analyzing her hair, I explained to her that she had some breakage, and more than likely, it was due to the blond color she had in her hair. I was so embarrassed when she replied, "Hmmm, that's funny, because I'm a natural blond." Second guessing myself at this point, I got through the cut as best as I could. Not to mention, there was hair everywhere as she did not have on a cutting cape. My old friend Wendell from Dudley use to always tell me, "When you are uncomfortable, it's usually because you're learning." I certainly had a lot to learn!

I will admit it was hard to get adjusted to working for someone after working for myself for many years. I also now had a supervisor. I got written up almost immediately.

Working for myself, I would typically get to work in the morning the same time my client would arrive, and that was considered being on time. However, at Chakras, if my first client was at 8:30 am, I was expected to be there 30 minutes before to get my station set up before my client arrived. I also remember doing my first head of partial highlights. I thought I did a wonderful job, but a few days later, I got in trouble again because the client came back because some of my foils bled and she was not happy about it. In due time, I finally got what I wanted, advance education!

Once I began to catch on to things, I got pretty busy. Now that I was a commission stylist who got paid bi-weekly, I had to work hard. I still worked at Salon Envy servicing my regular clients, so I was splitting my week between the two salons. To my surprise, it was never an issue making it until pay day because the tips I made on average were usually between $20 and $30 per client. I made about $300 to $400 weekly in tips alone. It's amazing how some clients don't know you should tip your stylist; some tip a dollar or two, and some don't tip at all! I had pretty good balance working with two different clienteles. As stressful as it would get learning so many new things, it was always good to go back to Salon Envy where I could be back in my comfort zone.

Weeks later, I would find out that I'd been fired at Chakras, but then, I found out that it was an accident. Two things happened. The first thing was the older lady who had the crush, now had it out for me, and when a client had a problem with something I did that didn't meet their expectation, the owner Sheila told them to just talk to me, but instead, I was fired due to miscommunication. Next, there was a new floor manager who was eager to flex his authority, and when I came in late, one too many times, he took full advantage of his position and fired me for real. I remember him being so serious that I couldn't stop laughing. I'm always amazed at how some people can take themselves so seriously. I knew I was there because I wanted to be there and not because I needed to be there.

    I remained at Salon Envy for the next three years, and became good friends with everyone there, especially the owner Lori Carter. I told Lori when I first came that I would more than likely, open another salon at some point, but it wouldn't be for a couple of years. When that time finally came, bad things began to occur. Not only did Lori's disposition change. There were also a few clients who treated me like I was homeless and thought I should've been so grateful that I was able to work in such a "nice salon" as they put it. I honestly felt these comments had some racists undertone to them, but it also got me recharged to do something phenomenal, and that's just what I did. I really wanted to stay at Salon Envy, until I was finished building my newest salon, but I had to leave as the tension began to thicken every day. After all, I knew I was a boss, and now I was about to show a few people why. Pardon my redundancy, but again, one of the best ways to get even with people is to be successful.

After leaving Salon Envy, a client of mine told me about a nice little salon, Simply Beautiful. It was the first time I'd worked on the east side, and although it was very small, the people were wonderful and had good energy! It was my pleasure to work with this team that consisted of Deanna, Tiffany, and the owner Kayla Slade.

Have you ever met someone in one place just by chance, and at some other point in life find that, that same person would play a role in your life that you'd never imagine? Well, there were two people like that in the next part of the journey I was about to embark. The first person came to enquire about working at Simply Beautiful. She was with another girl, but the way she walked down the center of the salon as if she were the wife of King Jaffe Jaffer from *Coming to America*, the other girl just vanished in the background. What I remember hearing her say most was that there were not enough mirrors in the salon for her to be able to work there. She said, "I need to be able to look at myself allllll day," as she pranced out of the door kind of disrespectfully. I couldn't decide if she was joking, and it was hard for me to imagine anybody really being that self-absorbed, but this would not be the last time we would meet.

The other person would be brought to my attention by one of my clients one day. She told me that a good friend of hers, who was a very talented stylist wanted to work with me. When I asked what his name was, she said Preston. Next, I asked if he were gay, but then I changed my question, and asked if he was "flamboyantly gay?" She answered, "well he does wear makeup." I then said, "absolutely not." I never had a problem with gay stylists in any of my salons. I was simply at a place where I was just a little fed up with stereotypical images in movies or television which type casted male hair stylists. Little did I know, both of these stylists would play major roles in my new salon, The Industry Salon Studio, as well as for the rest of my life!

10

Evolution of the Industry Salon Studio

Building my third salon, The Industry Salon Studio, was altogether different. It was located in Revolution Mill Studios, the same building as Salon Envy, I'd recently left. It was an old cotton mill that was now being remodeled and was also the talk of the town. The big difference was all I had to do was design the place. They "built to suite" each space. What wasn't so different was the fact that once again, I was doing a lot all at the same time, as if I had not learned from my experience with Scott Bonds Salon, and I was now engaged to an incredibly beautiful, young woman.

My new fiancé', Kelly Forrest, whose intelligence rivaled her external beauty, spoke five different languages which was very impressive to me. I remember telling my friend Harold about this beautiful woman I met who worked at the bank. He said, "yeah, I know exactly who you are talking about. She's Puerto Rican, right?" I said, "No, I don't think so. I'm pretty sure her last name was Forrest, and I don't believe that's Puerto Rican bro." He said he always heard her speaking Spanish, and that's why he thought that. I can also remember telling him that I had to wait until the right time to make a real move because I knew she was special, and I wanted to be totally honest with her about everything. I wasn't going to play any games with her. I always say that I chose my first wife, but God chose my second wife.

During this time, we were also planning our future as husband and wife as I was working on opening this new salon. I also purchased a new house that was almost 4000 sq. ft. and about $400,000. I was diligently working on my dream life. Not only did I want to have a house my children could be proud of, but I also wanted to have a family complete with healthy children, a wife that loved me and had my back, good health, and be the owner of a few thriving businesses.

As I think back to this time, I honestly have no idea how I was able to handle all of this at the same time. Many nights, I would stand in my yard thanking God for all his blessings, as I always remembered my humble beginnings. To know where I'd come from, living in a two bed room apartment in the hood, and sharing one of those rooms with my brother and sister, to now having this incredible home was everything I ever imagined. Along with my two

Rottweilers, Marley and Rocco, that roamed the property, I was really living my dream.

Over the next couple of months, I enjoyed my time working at Kayla's salon, and I also worked hard finding the perfect equipment to make this place everything I wanted. Once again, I try to improve with every salon I design. This time, one of the biggest expenses were the shampoo bowls I found. I fell in love the first time I saw them! They were imported from Italy and cost almost $1200 a piece. I also had a new friend, Ryan Bolger, who owned Schneider Stone which is a granite company, and he really hooked me up with the most beautiful granite that came from South Africa. It just so happened that he had enough of this left from a previous job and was able to sell it to me as a remnant. I used it for the shampoo back bar as well as a cap for the styling stations. My mirrors were custom cut to 3 feet by 6 feet, then custom framed and stained in a dark brown to match the rest of the furniture, and they were then hung from the ceiling with a large link chain. The mirrors in my salons were my signature look. I found many fantastic accessories at the furniture store IKEA, one of my favorite places. From my previous experience with salon ownership, I learned I didn't have to spend top dollar on every single item. Investing money in the most important things that would be used very frequently such as, styling chairs, shampoo bowls, and reception/waiting area furniture was most important. My niche was to find unique and inexpensive things to complement and accessorize with like shelving, area rugs, wall sconces, etc.

      For the third time, I felt very accomplished. This, to me, was a very special salon. The location was top notch, and I wanted to have a very special team to match. Truthfully, I still had not given up on having a diverse staff, and I was willing to wait as long as I had to, to get the right people. I knew the chances of attracting White or Hispanic stylists would become slim if I started with hiring other Black stylists. I don't mean this in a bad way. Just as churches generally believe in the same Bible, but are still typically separated by race, culture, and sometimes status, so are many salons. I waited for an entire year before hiring my first stylist. She happened to be White, but just like before, she was a recent graduate, and I really wasn't in the position to help her build and grow. Eventually, I had to give in and start hiring the people who showed the greatest interest in being there. At the very top of that list was the young lady whom I'd previously met while working at Kayla's. This was the one who needed to look at herself all day while she worked. Due to the fact that a large part of this relationship was not so good, I will refer to her from this point on as The Peacock.

      Initially, my instincts told me to leave her alone. I'd already had some insight about who she was just by what I'd already witnessed with my own two eyes. She came by the salon several times as I told her I still was not hiring just yet. Of course, I didn't go into details as to why. However, she just kept inquiring. Then, one day as I was walking downtown, this green Honda Accord with tinted windows slowly pulls up near me and rolls the window down to talk. It was The Peacock. At this point though, I was a little happy to see her, although it was a little stalkerish. I had been in my salon just about a year now, and between the rent and salon bills along with the hefty mortgage I now had for my new house, she looked like a bag of Benjamin Franklins! After really taking the time to get to know her a little better, I didn't think she was as bad as I had imagined in the first place, just a little vain, which is relatively normal in this business. She ended up being the first stylist I hired to work at The Industry Salon Studio.

It didn't take long for The Peacock and me to bond at all. Turns out, we got along great! She had a very cool boyfriend she'd been dating for about five years, who would keep everyone in stitches with his sense of humor, and they both got along very well with my new wife. It wasn't long before the four of us were hanging out almost every weekend. We used to have a ball! Sometimes we would just hang out at our house, have a few drinks, play music, and just laugh to no end. We became so close that one evening after I left the salon, something happened, and she passed out while she was still working. Her client called me, and I rushed back as if I were the ambulance. When I returned, I couldn't help but to wonder why she told her client to call me? She said I was the first person that came to her mind. This just shows how close we'd become. We all got along so well I decided to introduce them to a couple of people in my inner circle.

One evening, I invited The Peacock and her boyfriend over to my friend, Ayesha's, house to meet her along with her husband Ike, who is also hilarious in his own right. The six of us had dinner. As we all sat on their screened in porch laughing and drinking, the idea was born to a take a trip to Jamaica. Suddenly, travel plans were in full effect. Ike had a good friend who was a travel agent, so we booked a trip to go to Ocho Rios, August of that year. It was a late anniversary gift for my wife, as we got married June 9th the prior year. It was also a late birthday trip for Ayesha, as her birthday was June 17th, and it just so happen that we would be there for The Peacock's birthday, which was August 7th. Everybody had something to celebrate, and we were all very excited.

While all of this was going on, I was still looking for talented and established stylists. The chemistry The Peacock and I had was phenomenal at this point, and I really wanted to hire others that would only enhance the dynamic we already had. She was very talented. She had a great clientele as she did a little bit of everything. She was the first person that was able to convince me that wrapping your client's hair and placing a plastic cap on it after flat ironing it, really made a difference. I didn't know at that time that it was called a silk wrap, but I was so impressed with the results, I jokingly started calling the plastic cap we used a Peacock Bag! In the 90's, some stylists used Saran Wrap the same way.

As I was doing one of my clients one day, she mentioned that she had, "a friend that really wants to work with you, really bad." I said, "Let me guess. His name is Preston." She looked at me as if I was a psychic, and said, "Yes! How did you know that?" I told her his name had been brought to my attention several times, but I just couldn't see having a transgender stylist working in my salon, so I had to pass, once again. After she left however, I started wondering why this guy's name kept being brought up to me and if there was something more to it. I had to wonder if there was some purpose I was unaware of that God kept bringing this name to me.

Anyway, I called my client, who knew him, to get his contact information. I informed her that I'd changed my mind, and I thought I should meet him in person. He called me almost immediately, and we set a day and time for him to come to the salon so we could meet. I told The Peacock that I was thinking about giving him a chance potentially, but she didn't seem too excited. I believed that she may have had the same concern as myself, and she did not want to upset the chemistry we had.

A few days later, I had two potentially new stylists to interview, Chris Galloway was the first. He was a very fun energetic stylist. The interview went well, and I hired him. The next person to meet was Preston Crenshaw. Preston walked in with a Gucci hand bag held by a hand with long, pink nails, and black, stiletto boots. I thought to myself, *what have I got myself into*?! As he came in, we sat in two of the styling chairs and began to talk. I told him I'd heard a lot of great things about him, as he returned the compliment. After we talked for a while, I said to him that I really wanted to give him a chance, but I wanted to know if he could possibly "tone it down just a little bit?" He paused for a minute, then swung his hair, as it was flawless, then said, "when people see me, they want what I have. I am my best advertisement, so when you say can I tone it down, what do you mean exactly?" It doesn't happen often, but momentarily, I was at a loss for words. Then, I responded and said to him, "As I think about you working here, I have to ask myself if I'm concerned with how the clients are going to feel about you being here, or am I more concerned with how I will feel about you working here? And if it was the latter, then that would suggest that I'm not really who I say I am. I take pride in being very non-judgmental, and with that being said, I'm going to give you a chance, and we will just see how things work out." As he left that day, my phone started ringing immediately because he started telling everyone he was going to be working with me at The Industry Salon Studio. He was so excited, and I felt great that I was able to get out of my own way and make someone else happy in doing so.

11

Divas, Egos, and Attitudes

After bringing Preston along with Chris on the still developing team, things had been going very well. The trip to Jamaica with The Peacock and our significant others was nearing. However, I was beginning to notice a change happening with her. It started to seem like she was suddenly against me any time the opportunity came. It was as if she wanted everyone to know that she was better than anyone else in the salon. She always did her best to make sure all eyes were on her, and every conversation was about her. I couldn't put my finger on what it was exactly, but I tried to find the words to explain what was happening to my wife, Ayesha and Ike. All I could tell them was they would know what I was talking about as soon as we all got together.

As each day passed, and our departure date got closer, I began dreading the entire trip. All I could tell the rest of the group was I think we made a big mistake. Although the Peacock and I had been working together for a good while at this point, I still had not met several of her clients. There were many times one of her clients would come in for the first time and mention how they had heard so many good things about me. It always seemed to hit a nerve in her. I was so befuddled by this behavior, as I always spoke so highly of her, and pumped her up to everybody. By this time in my career, I was looking for a way out of working behind the chair. I used to tell her that I would want her to take over the salon once I got to where I aspired. I truly only wanted the best for her. Prior to this strange behavior, I really had considered her as one of my best friends. This really bothered me. Suddenly, she was becoming my greatest opposition.

    The day had finally arrived for us to depart to the beautiful Jamaica! August 5th, two days away from The Peacocks birthday, we arrived, and everyone was beginning to see what I'd been saying. She made every step we took while we were there about herself. One of the most memorable things that happened was on the day of her birthday; she was expecting to get a popular watch by Michael Kor. Instead, she received a no named brand watch, and she pouted the entire day. She really didn't even want to wear it. The other thing that happened was what defined our entire trip. Later that evening of her birthday, we all planned a dinner outside of a very nice restaurant. It was so hot that evening, that it was really uncomfortable to be outside. As we all sat waiting for our server to come take our order, The Peacock talked about herself the entire time. At this point, everyone was very much over all of this. Suddenly, without any sign or warning, Ike gets up without saying one word and leaves the table. Although at that moment, none of us knew why he did this, it was the funniest thing ever! When we got back to the room, Ike said he just couldn't take it anymore. He said, "I was out there sweating, and I was hot as hell, and I wasn't about to be out there listening to her shit all night!" We still managed to have an ok time, but when we returned, Ike never associated with The Peacock again. As for me and The Peacock's friendship, it began going downhill fast.

Once we returned, The Peacock blamed me for Ayesha and Ike not continuing the friendship with her. She never thought it could've been anything she did. Meanwhile, Chris and Preston got along just fine in our absence. At this point in the salon, there were only two chairs open, and soon, those would be filled. In time, communication with The Peacock was rare. It was such bad energy in the salon. She would be as nice as she possibly could be to everyone else, but she would totally ignore me. I truly learned what passive aggressive behavior was from this experience.

As the owner of a salon, or any type of business, it was essential for me to remove bad energy from my environment immediately! Bad energy is like a terminal illness, and if you give it too much time, it will eat away at your business like a cancer! Unfortunately, when you own a booth rent salon, you sometimes tend to endure more than you should, for the sake of the bottom dollar.

Over the next few months, I would eventually fill the remaining two chairs. Although the Peacock threatened to leave if I brought her on, a very talented stylist name Lindsey would join us. She said she would see Lindsey out sometimes, and she would never really speak to her, although they knew one another. I didn't allow that to stop me from hiring her. Lastly, Lisa joined our team just as Chris decide to leave after only a few months. She was the perfect replacement. She brought a lot of fire to the salon in many different ways. She was a very strong minded, opinionated, pro Black woman with such an incredible figure that men would stop by just to look at her. She was definitely a force to be reckoned with. Actually, guys would often inquire about many of the stylists that worked there. We not only had a good looking team, but this was also the most talented group I'd ever had in any of my salons. The down side was that nobody seemed to care about anyone but themselves. Just as in my other salons, it was still important to try to assist the team in bonding on some level. This proved to be the most challenging thing ever!

Although the chairs were now full and the money was there, I began to experience something I'd never experienced ever before. Suddenly, I seemed to be struggling doing things that in the past came easily. The biggest adjustment was learning how to do many of the things I would see the other stylist doing with the flat iron. Doing the shorter styles was the thing I struggled with the most. I just couldn't seem to get the right curl, along with figuring out the right products, and the right amount of product as well. This was very different than working with the thermal curling irons I'd mastered long ago. I found myself lost. It was like I'd been wearing magic shoes for twenty years, and suddenly, they stopped working. As I previously mentioned, I don't ever need to be the best in my salon, but my confidence was gradually getting worse and worse.

  By this time, Preston and I had become great friends, and he would often try to show me certain things he thought would help me. He used to always tell me to just do it, and don't be scared. He was great at everything he did in the salon. Preston was also the only person I could trust on my team at this point and was very valuable to the entire salon. He seemed to always keep the mood of the salon in a fun place. As for me, it was never about me being scared. It's just that I've always been such a perfectionist, and I simply expected my work to be on a certain level that I seemingly was not achieving at this point. As a stylist, I knew I should never be fearful of a challenge in my chair. I understood that anytime I felt uncomfortable was a sign of growth. It was necessary to reach back in my mental arsenal to remember skills and techniques I thought I may never need or use again. It was time to get some advanced education.

The next few years would prove to get even harder over time. You often hear people tell you God is testing you. You also hear people say that things will get better, but it never seems to end sometimes. A few things that happened during this time would prove to be important in my continuing evolutionary process.

One day, as I was walking out of the building where my salon was located. I wasn't paying attention, and before I knew it, I flew down seven or eight stone steps, head first, with my morning Starbucks coffee, and everything else I was carrying! Able to get my hands in front of my face to break my fall, the force of landing like that made me feel something terribly wrong in my shoulder, instantly. As I laid there for a few, I thanked God that I didn't bust my face wide open and wondered if anyone saw what just happened. I knew there was no way I would stand up and everything would be ok. In that moment, I thought about the Aflac sales rep that had been coming by my salon for the last few months encouraging me to buy supplemental insurance and how I kept putting it off. I knew I was in trouble. Up until this moment, I'd never been sick or hospitalized for any reason in almost twenty years, but the day had finally come. I tried to go in my salon once I got myself together, but my arm just didn't feel right, so I drove myself to the emergency room just around the corner to get the official word on what was wrong. Turns out, I tore my rotator cuff and would need to have surgery to repair it. I would be out of work for two and a half months!

It is said that the average person is one pay check from being homeless. For me, I couldn't imagine being out of work for almost three months and how I would manage to pay my mortgage of almost $3000 a month, along with my car payment, salon rent and utilities, home utilities, and a host of other expenses as well. All I could do was to plan as best as possible and do a lot of praying. I had a small nest egg I was able to use, and my salon was still full, so I certainly had to count my blessings. Truthfully, had it not been for my father, I probably would've never made it through this time period.

Though I didn't really have a team in my salon I could feel comfortable with in my complete absence, I didn't have a choice. I knew I could count on Preston to keep me up to date on anything he thought I should be aware of, and by this time, there was a new, young talent who I had formed a pretty good relationship with named Ayanna. She was one of the most responsible stylists I'd ever met, in addition to being one of the most talented as well. I must say she was one of the few people that offered me some advice to help me improve my flat ironing skills. One of the things I admired most about her was she always looked great at work. Many stylists don't realize the importance of personal appearance. She did. She was also a former salon owner, so she knew how to handle her business. I decided to leave her in charge of the retail sales, and I asked the rest of my staff to keep the salon up as if it were their own. I wasn't very confident that this would go well. I could only imagine how things would go in my absence.

It didn't take long to find out just how right I was, as Ayanna called to inform me that The Peacock was selling my retail, keeping the money, and replacing my retail when the sales reps would visit. When Ayanna told her that I left her in charge, and that she was to collect all the retail money, The Peacock told her that she "had to eat, just like Scott," so she wasn't giving her any money and would continue to do what she wanted to do. I was furious when I heard about this! Once I was able to come to the salon, we had a meeting, and this was probably the first of three times I was going to let The Peacock go, but I always felt bad because I always remembered the nice person she was real deep down inside, and I almost felt sorry for her. When I spoke to her about what she had done, she started crying, and once again, I simply got soft and let her stay.

Once I made it back to work, things still seemed to be exactly the same. I still did not enjoy working in my own salon. The energy was simply off, and it drove me insane. Ironically, if Preston had not been there during this time, I certainly would have closed the doors long ago.

12

The Storm Before the Calm

After the surgery, it wasn't long before I was back on a regular schedule, and all the stress I'd left before my surgery was right there waiting on me to return. Things really got crazy during the local university's, North Carolina A&T, homecoming weekend. During this time, everyone is typically very busy, and since everyone in the salon was what I believed the most talented in the area, we were all super busy. As I walked in first thing that morning, The Peacock decided that she was going to have an assistant for the day. I would never have a problem with anyone having an assistant, but I would have liked the respect and consideration of having a prior conversation. Anyway, I decided it wasn't worth saying anything. Later in the day, she had her assistant get the two of them something to eat. She certainly wasn't going to let the rest of us benefit from her assistant. After the assistant returned with the food, she sat the food on the counter in the dispensary area where the color was mixed, along with other salon related tasks. When I went to mix color for my client, I placed the food on the top of the refrigerator to move it out of the way. About ten minutes after that, The Peacock went to the area and shouted completely across the salon," Scott, did you put my food on top of the refrigerator?" I responded "Yes" as everyone was looking to see why she was raising her voice. She went on to say, "Don't be putting my food on the top of no refrigerator. My momma don't even put my food on top of no refrigerator!" Everyone was just standing or sitting in shock, wondering why she was upset. Meanwhile, my silly friend Preston peeked around the mirror that divided our station and jokingly said, "Yo bruh, you gonna let her disrespect you in your salon like that?" I would later deal with it, but I've trained myself over the years to never react impulsively and or emotionally. I wasn't willing to stoop down to her level and pour fuel on the fire. I would, however, handle it after careful thought. I knew it was time to ask her to leave. To allow this behavior, without any consequence, would have sent the wrong message to the rest of the staff and could have set the stage for recurring treatment.

    Honestly, after telling her that she had to go, I still felt bad and told her that perhaps God placed the two of us in each other's life to make us better somehow, and if she wanted to stay, we probably could work through this as well, but she made it sound like every big time hair salon in the continental U.S. was trying to get her to come work with them. I wasn't surprised. I hoped, if nothing else, it would show her how I still genuinely had a lot of love for her, although we hadn't been getting along. Unfortunately, we never reconciled our relationship. However, I am happy to say today she is doing very well and is creating the life she wants for herself and her family. I knew this experience was one of the many necessary moments that would help me continue to evolve and grow.

Now that the biggest part of my stress was gone, I once again enjoyed coming to work. During this time, I was also informed by Boz about an opportunity working for the North Carolina Board of Cosmetic Arts. Unknown to me at the time, he was now Chairman of the Board. I applied, interviewed and received the position. It was said that I was the first African American to be an inspector in Guilford County, and it wasn't long before it was clear to me that there would be some who would have to get use to this. Once I walked in to a very high-end salon to do their inspection. I was very patient as well as polite. I stood to the side of the owner's station, not to intrude, but still be visible, hoping I could introduce myself, and proceed to do my job. She turned to me with disgust and told me that if I wanted to speak with her, I would need to see the receptionist and wait. I politely informed her that, "I just wanted to introduce myself." I continued, "My name is

Scott Bonds, and I'm with the North Carolina Board of Cosmetic Arts. I'm here to do your inspection." To see the look on her face as I proceeded to go through every nook and cranny of her salon was priceless. Needless to say, she became very nice to me before it was all said and done. In the end, it was a bit too much maintaining my salon and working for the state. They needed my job with the state to be my priority, but I still had a business.

With stylist coming and going, I became behind on the rent and was constantly struggling to keep everything current. My income suddenly was half of what I'd been making for many years, and it was taking a toll on all aspects of my life. This is when I really learned more about faith. It tends to be very easy to say you have faith when things are not so bad, but when things get really bad, your faith is really tested. It was as if God was trying to move me forward, but I loved my salon so much, and knew all of its potential as the building we were located in was getting closer and closer to completing the $75 million renovation that I'd been there to see for the last nine years. It was just about to be complete, so I simply didn't want to close the doors. I would, however, witness a few miracles in my life in the days to come, but the miracle I witnessed, in my now best friend, Preston's life, would be the greatest of all.

I was really in the struggle of trying to survive, maintain my home, keep my sanity, and fight off bill collectors. I began stepping up my spirituality. It had been my experience that sometimes God must allow you to get so low, that you realize only He can pull you back up. I was constantly reminded of how He was looking over the things occurring in my life. Once I had to make the decision to pay a bill, but I knew I also had another that had consequences attached to it, if it wasn't paid. I paid the first, without any idea how I would pay the other, and as I returned to my salon, I checked the mail, and there was a greeting card size envelope with my name on it. When I opened it, there was a money order for $200 from a former stylist who owed me money! It had been well over two years, and I never expected to get anything from her. There in my time of need, and borderline desperation, it showed up! More importantly, it had the most heartfelt note written letting me know that she appreciated all that I did. It really meant a lot, was very timely, and there was more to come.

    A client called me at the salon one day and wanted to make an appointment. I had not seen her in about six or seven years. She wore her hair in a short clipper cut and didn't require much. As she sat there while I was cutting her hair, we discussed differences we had in the past, and she wanted to apologize. As she was leaving, she wrote a check and handed it to me. When I unfolded the check, it read $500! I immediately called her to tell her that it was not necessary, and she should come get the check. She laughed as she refused, said "I love you," and hung up the phone. I haven't seen her since. I knew God was totally monitoring my life.

And the angels just seemed to keep coming. A client of mine. early in my career, called. She told me one day that something just made her think of me, and she just wanted to know if I was alright? She knew my wife and I recently had a son, Sai Noah Bonds who was now two years old, and asked if there was anything we needed. I just kind of laughed and said, "I'm good," and we went on to have a good conversation. She had been living in California with her husband, daughter, and stepson, but was now back in the area. After hanging up, she called me back saying she wanted to bring me something. When she came by, she handed me an envelope. She said something in her spirit told her to do this. Since I didn't want her to feel sorry for what I was going through, I didn't really tell her anything, but when I opened the envelope, she'd given me $1000! There were others who would do the same.

After having such experiences, whenever people close to me ask for financial help, and need to borrow money, I cannot burden them with worrying how to pay me back. I almost feel obligated to just give them the money.

13

The Greatest Miracle

Though I fought, closing the doors of The Industry Salon was seemingly getting closer, but not before the greatest miracle was to occur. During this time, Preston and I had become very close, and our daily routine was to go to his house after work with a few other friends and just talk. I will confess becoming close friends with Preston made me dig deeper into who I really was. It took time before I was completely relaxed going out to eat with just the two of us. Eventually, I did become comfortable with our friendship, and it didn't really matter who thought what. I invited him anyplace I was going and never let anyone talk bad about him. I knew first hand he had my back in the same way.

One day Preston started telling me about a few spiritual things he had been experiencing. He went on to tell me that it was as if God was calling on him to make a change in his life. Now, this was a shock. This was a person who had gradually become a full transgender person over a ten year period. After sharing his recent experiences with me, he suddenly, and with great excitement said to me, "I need to talk to your father!" I said no problem. He repeated himself again, "I'm serious Scott. I need to talk to him ASAP!" Again, I said, "I got you. I will call him as soon as I leave." That following Monday, my father and Preston met at my house, had some coffee, and talked for a couple of hours. At the end of the conversation, my father invited us to come to the masjid, as they invited non-Muslims every third Saturday, to find out the truth about the religion of Islam, as well as ask any questions they may have. This would truly be a day I would never forget.

Preston was super anxious and super nervous all at the same time. The only clothes he had were women clothes, so he borrowed a few things from his father and brother. As we sat there, to both of our surprise, not only were there mostly White people there, but the person leading the event was also a White person. He'd recently became Muslim just a few years ago and was so well versed. Some looked at him as a local scholar. His name was Issa, which is Jesus in Arabic. He was humble and very thorough. He introduced himself as "a redneck from the country" who was led to the fold of Islam.

Soon, it was time for the Muslims to make their prayer, so the non-Muslims went to the back and talked amongst one another. Preston expressed to me that he wanted to talk to Issa and ask a few questions. I told him to just go talk to him. After the prayer was over, we proceeded to go speak with Issa further. Preston began by saying, "I've been living my life as a woman for the past ten years, and I know that God didn't put me here to live like this." He went on to say, "I felt Him calling me but wasn't sure what I was supposed to do." He explained how he attempted to go to church, but he knew that wasn't it. He confessed after hearing everything that day, he knew this was the place God was leading him. Next, in a very pressing yet excited voice, he said, "What do I need to do to become Muslim?" Brother Issa explained to him what needed to be done, and that once he took his Shahadah (bearing witness that there is no God but Allah, and Muhummad is his last and final messenger), he would be forgiven for his sins up to that moment and would start fresh. Preston said, "Ok, I'm ready. I want to do it right now." I said to him, "Yo, are you sure you don't want to think about this just a little?" He responded and said, "No Scott. I have to do this right now!"

    I think my father was more excited than anyone that day. Being in that moment, I also re-dedicated to Islam as well which was one of the greatest wishes of my father. He, along with the others, shouted "Takbir, Allahuakbar," meaning God is great! Preston said he instantly felt a burden lifted off of him. As for me, the burden was just about to increase. I've always been very spiritual but never saw myself to be or become religious. However, Preston was all in. He gave away all of his clothes, purses, and any jewelry that was feminine. He gradually cut off all his hair and began making every prayer on time five times a day. His salon schedule revolved completely around Islam. He no longer engaged in any foolishness, and he began studying the Quran. He even started to learn how to read and speak Arabic. I wasn't surprised by his commitment because I always told people that Preston was very intelligent and not to be thrown off by his appearance as a transgender person. I knew that it wouldn't be long before he would stop doing hair all together, as a Muslim man is not supposed to touch a woman that is not his wife.

Everyone was in shock seeing the new Preston. He changed his name to Yusef. He lost most of his friends, and his family thought he'd gone crazy. Most people thought it was just a phase. I assured them, whenever I had the chance, that this was a permanent change, and they would never see the old Preston. Eventually, as I expected, he told me that he was going to have to stop doing hair. Although I was fully expecting this moment, it still hurt very much. He was my absolute closest friend, and I saw that we were about to slowly drift apart. He had become a truly religious person, and that just wasn't who I was. Furthermore, as I mentioned earlier, he was the most positive energy in the salon, and with his absence, I knew I would be closing soon. I was sad to hear that he would be retiring from doing hair, but I was so incredibly happy for who he'd become. He literally sacrificed everything and started his entire life over. I reflected on how we met, how bad he wanted to work with me, and how I was a vehicle for him to arrive where he was. I was happy to have been a part of his journey. Closing the Industry Salon was no longer a sad thing. It had served its purpose.

Preston was that one person I had grown to count on to help keep up my spirits, but now as each day passed, our paths seemed to drift further and further apart, at least momentarily.

With my life feeling like it was falling apart again, I felt like I was about to have a nervous breakdown. I was often torn between wanting to be alone and wanting to talk to someone. Each time I tried to reach out to someone to vent, it seemed like they were too busy.

One day, it occurred to me that this was God trying to get me to work things out through Him. However, I know when you take the necessary time in silence, whether it's in meditation, or simply riding in your car without any music and in complete silence, the voice that dwells within all of us, can be heard more clearly. Typically, when I listen to that voice, I find that things work out for the best. Many of us have good friends, but believe me, there is nobody that cares about you, as much as you care about you. I realized that everyone has something they are dealing with, and sometimes their time is limited because they have their own lives. I had to learn to go within.

Although I was at peace with closing, I still made a

few last attempts to stay in that space. I came up with an idea to redo the salon and make it into a high-end barber lounge called the Lion's Den, but after weighing the pros and cons, the risks were too great. I loaded all of my equipment onto a trailer, which seemed to take an entire day, and put my things in storage. I really didn't feel like I would ever open another salon again. This salon took more out of me than any other salon I'd ever owned, and it really made me lose a tremendous amount of the passion I once had. However, I was smart enough to not sell all my things in haste. After all, I'd felt this way before about not ever wanting to open another salon, and it didn't last long. I ended up finding a salon around the corner from where my first salon, The Right Angle, was located. Until I could regroup, I simply needed to be a booth renter and take time to see what I was supposed to do next.

14

Rest and Recovery

The new location where I was working was just around the corner from where I recently closed. It was easy for my clients to find, but most importantly, it was like coming home. It was in the same building that I'd opened my first and most successful salon, The Right Angle, but on the other side of the shopping complex. There were still several salons that were there twenty years ago, and it was like being around old friends again. It made me think deeper about what these other salon owners and other business owners had been doing over the last two decades, and what the many other Black owned salons I'd seen open and close over the years were doing wrong. One thing I can say is there is value in being small in size and very successful versus trying to be too big and failing under the pressures that sometimes come along with expansion.

    Working at MOD Studio was rest and recovery for me. It allowed me to simply be a normal stylist, pay my rent, and keep it moving. I've always said to be a good leader you must be able to be a good follower when the leadership is good. I made sure I still took care of the salon as if it were my own. I stayed on top of all the responsibilities given to me as well. The team consisted of two Black stylists and two White stylists. It said something good to me that the salon not only had a multicultural staff, but it was also multiculturally owned. I, at least, knew the women who owned the salon were strong, empowered and intelligent in their own individual ways. They all previously worked together at another salon for several years before deciding to leave and open a place together. Diverse ownership can be beneficial, as long as all agreements between the parties involved are clearly understood, as well as documented. This salon proved that.

    As much as I admired MOD having a multicultural staff, I still knew it could be very challenging. However, my time there allowed me to learn many things about ownership. It also gave me a different perspective about how to interact with coworkers as a salon owner.
I've learned not to judge or assume things about people many times and being at MOD continued this lesson. There were people and stylist that might appear to be racist or not

like you, but I found that if I simply opened my mouth and talked to a person, I discovered we had more in common than I assumed.

At the end of the day, what I enjoyed most with MOD Studio was that the people I worked with proved to me that I wasn't crazy after all! All the things I'd believed to be possible in a salon, they were doing. They kept the salon clean throughout the day; everyone folded towels, and most importantly, having a salon with diversity was an everyday thing. This kept me hopeful.

15

When the Pieces Fall in Place

After working at MOD for about seven months, I started feeling like I needed something else. Not that I wasn't happy being a booth renter and only being responsible for myself. I knew that as a stylist, I was most comfortable in an atmosphere that I was responsible for providing to the people that visited my salon. Still, I didn't want to jump right back into becoming a salon owner, and I knew if and when that time came around again, it would need to be something different. As soon as I started at MOD, another salon owner, who knew me from my first salon I had in the same building, offered me a place he owned there, and he offered me a very attractive lease, but the timing was all wrong. I knew God would let me know when to make my next move.

The time finally came. The owner of a salon just a

few doors down from where I was presently working contacted me to inform me, she was about to close. Months prior, I remember walking into that same space thinking to myself that it had a pretty nice set up and what I might do to enhance it if it were mine. I actually decided to take a look when I heard it would soon be available, simply out of curiosity.

    I contacted the leasing agent for this property to schedule an appointment to take a closer look. It was a lot smaller than I imagined, and initially, I couldn't see how I could make this into something as special. I also wasn't certain what I could create in this space that would be different yet still profitable. I decided to ask the leasing agent if I could have the key so that I could be in the space alone to see if anything came to mind. I went back several times while I had the keys, as I kept walking back and forth thinking how many stylists I would need to make it a good situation. I knew that I didn't want to have too many chairs, as most salons struggle to fill their chairs. Then the idea came to me!

    My oldest son, Scotty, was now 26 years old and a very talented chef. I always wanted to help him with his business. He was rapidly making a name for himself. The idea came to me to explore the possibilities of combining our businesses in one space to create what I would eventually call a Salon Café. He had already started by selling cookies in my previous salon, eventually moved to cupcakes, and then food dishes. He was selling in my salon as well as other salons in the area. As I went back into the space I was considering, the vision began to take shape. I ran the idea by my son, and he was very excited and on board. With that concept in mind, I was now able to go in and sketch out a design. The owner really wanted to lease the space out as soon as possible and agreed to a very good lease. He also let me know that he'd be willing to sell the space when and if I was ready to purchase. This was exactly what I wanted to hear. The only thing left to do now was to find the money to make this a reality.

I generally don't like to borrow money from anyone, but I had to humble myself enough to ask for help. I decided to ask two people to loan me $1000. Both agreed without hesitation. In addition, my father, who has never told me no since I've been alive, also agreed to give me some financial assistance.

 Now that I had a budget, I was now on my way. I had to see how I could pull this thing together with only $5000. I knew someone who did the type of work that would be needed to make it everything I imagined, but when the estimate came back at $6000, I knew I was about to have to learn a lot of things on my own. I wasn't even sure if I had that much left in me to get it done. It had been years, and I was a lot older. I also now had a wife and toddler in my life I had to consider. The most amazing thing is that I constantly kept getting signs that this was exactly what I was supposed to be doing, and it was as if I was being divinely guided throughout the entire process!

To my advantage, MOD Studio had decided that they would be closing when their lease was over in just a couple of months, so the timing of me starting this project was perfect. I had observed the work ethic and other habits of my co-workers, and I knew that if I could somehow get them to believe in my vision, I would have my dream team immediately. Heather was a young, White stylist, that I had grown to love. She was very enthusiastic about her craft, and I used to joke with her all the time, telling her that she had what I called Chick-fil-a customer service. She was the kind of nice that I simply could not be. I mentioned to her what I was working on, but she didn't jump right on board immediately, so I really wasn't sure if she would come with me or not. Then, there was Nikki. I really loved her work ethic as well, and she had a terrific range of things she could do. The fact that she was a single mother raising her soon to be teenage son, made me see even more how special she was. Both Nikki and Heather were great colorists, and that too was very important to me to have in my salon. When I approached the conversation with Nikki about joining me, she informed me that she was planning to move to Virginia because there was a good opportunity there for both her and her son. I did what I could do to sell her on coming with me, but it didn't seem to work. She was, however, very supportive and told me she shared the opportunity with one of her best friends, Ebony, who I'd known indirectly from another salon she worked in that my good friend Harold used to own. I didn't know her that well, but I would run into her from time to time at Whole Foods, and she always seemed to have good energy. I decided to reach out to her to see what she thought. She met me at what was to be my new salon to talk. I walked her around with a sketch of my concept, explaining my vision as best I could. I remember her telling me that she already knew it was going to be very nice, as she had seen my other salons. It made me feel good that she believed in me, and she said she would be happy to join once it was complete. Since I wasn't certain about Heather still, I reached out to a stylist that reached out to me about working at my previous salon just as I was in the process of closing. She too, had some bad experiences and was closing her salon as well. When she met me at the space, she too had nothing but great things to say about what I'd done in the past and that she would also be happy to join. She was also very talented, and I knew she would be an asset to the salon as well. Both of them told me they would definitely join me when I was ready to open. This was shaping up to be the best thing ever.

    Because I only planned to have four stations, and I now had three filled including myself, I really wanted another male stylist to balance things. Because Ebony previously worked with Harold, and I knew Harold was one of the best stylists I had at Scott Bonds Salon, he was definitely my top choice to fill the last remaining chair. When I called him, I told him what I was putting together, that there was no pressure, and there would be absolutely no love lost if he was happy where he was presently working. He said he would think about it, and he would let me know something soon.

One thing I knew for sure that my plans meant nothing, and that God's plan is all that really mattered. The only thing you can do is adjust when the plan is altered from what you had in mind. I already had commitments from two stylists but still wasn't sure about Heather or Harold at this point. One day as we began to get closer to the date MOD was closing, I heard Heather say to one of her clients, "Hopefully Scott will let me come with him to the new salon he's opening." I said, "Excuse me?" She said, "Yes, I was just telling my client about the salon you are working on, and I was hoping you still wanted me to join you?" That moment made me feel so good, mainly because once again, it showed me she had confidence in what I was doing, and in this case, she hadn't even known me that long. I now had my dream team. I knew Harold was uncertain about what he wanted to do, so I didn't press him. I knew that if it was meant for us to work together again, it would happen in due time.

Now I really had to turn up the steam on getting this salon up and running. One of the biggest differences between building this salon versus the others I'd built was that this time I had a full staff waiting to move in, and I had no time to waste.

16

What You Don't See…

Now that I had a full staff, I'd given my word that the new salon would be ready in just a couple of months. I had to make serious progress and had to do it fast. I estimated all of the materials I would need to do the build. Again, I knew what I wanted the end result to be, but there were several things I would have to teach myself. I didn't really know of all the materials I would need.

Lowes Home Improvement delivered all the materials I ordered, and there before me, sat a big stack of sheetrock, nails, screws, 2x4's, and various other materials. Initially, I planned to put an entire new floor down, and even went through the difficult process of selecting the perfect flooring. I didn't have a truck or a willing friend at the time to pick it up, so I drove my BMW and put as many boxes as I could carry in the back seat and trunk, and I drove back and forth until I had them all. Later that month, one of my very good friends I mentioned earlier, Ray Jones, stopped by to check out the space and gave me several great ideas. Amongst many things, he shared with me that day, he thought the existing floors looked great and recommended I keep them. After considering all that he shared, I decided he was right about the floor, especially since it was going to save me about $1800, and a ton of sweat equity. He also recommended I use LED lighting, due to the efficiency and longevity. Lighting is very important in a salon or barber shop, as you need to be able to see color services in true day light type of lighting, and in barber shops, you must be able to clearly see from all angles free of shadows to provide the best cuts and overall services possible. He also had several different carpet squares in his storage building and said he would gladly give them to me. Lastly, he thought putting a glass door leading to the back of the salon would be a nice touch; he also had one to give me. I'm so appreciative for Ray. He has always been supportive of anything I've done during our thirty years of friendship.

 I took all the advice Ray had given me. Fortunately, I was able get my long-time friend Mike, who was by far the most knowledgeable person as far as construction was concerned and had a truck, to help me return the flooring I'd spent so much time picking out and picking up. He also helped me with a few things I was not familiar doing as well. Now, I had to get on the move. There was a guy I met while at the last salon's location, at Revolution Mill. His name was Marshall. I didn't know a lot about him, but again this was a person who always had great energy whenever I would see him. He was the head maintenance guy there, so I reached out to him to see if he knew of, or might be a carpenter, and would be willing to help me. He then told me he was not a carpenter, but he was a licensed electrical contractor, and he proved to be an awesome man. Marshall was always there when he said he would be, did great work, and charged me a very fair price. He was definitely one of the blessings during this process.

Now that I'd decided to keep the existing floor, it was only necessary for me to redo the entryway flooring that was badly water damaged. Just as the other flooring had taken a lot of time to select, so did this small but important 5x8 space as well. My daily schedule for the next two months consisted of me working at MOD Studio all day; then, I would change into my work clothes, just as I did in the beginning when building The Right Angle and working until the early hours the next morning building my latest vision.

After I was well into this project, both financially and physically, my son comes in one day, and out of the blue, he tells me that he doesn't think this is the right opportunity for him. I wouldn't even subject you to the words I used in this moment, as I was mad as the devil and very disappointed. From one angle, I certainly understood the potential uncertainty of going into a business situation like this during the same time his girlfriend was expecting their first child and my first grandson, but my gut felt like this was rooted in fear, so I talked to him for about thirty minutes that day, explaining how you have to step out on faith in business at certain times. I also reassured him that although I had no intention on babying him, I was still his dad, and I would never just let him flat out fail. I even had Ray talk with him to help him see I was simply laying the same ground work for him that his father did for him to make his future a little easier. Only after I relieved him of any financial risks was he back on board.

After the conversation with my son, I continued to work on the salon. I could truly see things even clearer after putting the first coat of paint on the walls. Not long after I had chosen a particular shade of purple as my central color did I received an email stating that the Pantone color of the year was that same shade of purple! That was just another sign assuring me that I was truly on the right track. This entire experience was very spiritual, and I felt divinely guided. This next task would be just one more very spiritual experience. I knew where I wanted to have the cooler for my son's gourmet desserts, but I had to figure out how to build the counter/bar so it would all flow well. It was like God was saying to me, "I have provided everything you need! Now build the salon!"

After teaching myself many new things, such as building a dryer bar I was very proud of, cutting, painting, and installing what seemed to be a million feet of base board, hanging kitchen cabinets after having put them all together and installing a sink and counter top, repairing the seal of the toilet that broke off, and building the shampoo bar, I was very close to being done. By this time, MOD had reached the end of their lease and closed the doors. Fortunately, Frank Price, the owner of a salon that practically opened almost when the development was first built thirty years ago, allowed my new team to work in his salon until I was ready to open. This would be another example of not judging people, without ever taking the time to get to know them. I knew Frank as we were both on the Advisory Board of the cosmetology department at GTCC where my old friend Morris 'Boz' Boswell was the department head. He would typically arrive at our orientation for the new students with his golfing attire; he would speak very candidly to the students and scare the hell out of them. It was always funny, but the things he would share with them was always very real. Anyway, working with him, I found that we had a lot in common, and he is one of the nicest guys ever. Along with myself, the new team temporarily working there for that time was a win win situation.

 However, I finally had to get the doors open. I'm a perfectionist, and therefore wanted everything to be complete upon opening, but I had to let my team get settled in and begin to work in this new and exciting environment. Heather was the first to move in, and Ebony was right afterwards. When I called the other stylist that told me she was definitely going to be joining us, I couldn't seem to reach her. When I finally received a text from her, it was telling me about her mother being ill and how things were so crazy and all. When I never heard back from her, I assumed plans changed, and she didn't really know how to tell me. I didn't question it because I believe everything happens for a reason. Amazingly, a few days later, Nikki, who was planning to move to Virginia with her son, decided that she would now stay in Greensboro and wanted to know if I still wanted her to work in the salon. I realized she didn't really understand, or maybe she didn't believe me, when I initially told her that she was a part of my Dream Team. This was again another sign that this was meant to be. Nikki finally came to join the team, and my dream was now complete. I've worked with many stylists over the years, but this was the first time I had people around me that cared for not only each other, but they also cared about me. Witnessing the team validated my most recent blessing, as I saw the love and true friendship, manifest before my very eyes.

17

Everything is Purposeful, Nothing Happens by Coincidence.

I'm a very open minded person and will typically give something a chance before flat out denying something because it's a little foreign to me. During a conversation with a longtime friend of mine, Nomvuyo Nxumalo, better known as Sunni, she asked me how I felt about people who are mediums or intuitives? If you are not familiar, it's a very spiritual, real and powerful thing. Just like mothers can feel and sense things about their children, people who have a broader sense of intuition can sometimes take that gift to another level and help others. After hearing all about Sunni's incredible experience, it was really on my mind, and I wanted to see for myself.

Later that day, I called another friend of mine, Ayisha Evans, who is one of Sunni's best friends. After only a few minutes into the conversation, she began to share with me her experience with the same intuitive. Once she finished telling me how good this guy was, I knew I had to see for myself! Immediately after hanging up the phone, I made my appointment.

The day finally came that I was to have what is commonly known as a reading. I wasn't quite sure what I was to do. I asked if I was to ask him a question or simply just listen? He informed me to allow him to read my energy and to ask questions later. Initially, he hit on a few things that kind of got my attention, but I still wasn't impressed. Suddenly, he told me that I was the kind of person that had a few different businesses and that I should be traveling around ministering to people. He then shared that I was also a very intuitive person as well. Without me ever mentioning anything about me writing a book, he told me that the book I am thinking about writing was the key to me going to the next level that I wanted so bad. He said I had a lot to share with people that would help many. When he said that, I wondered who in my tight circle of friends could he possibly have spoken to because I've said this exact thing several times. During the reading, he also gave me the ingredients to a spiritual bath to take. I listened, received the message that was coming through him, and followed instructions.

The next day, I had the house alone. After taking the bath he suggested, a day later, everything I had been trying to figure out about my book and how to complete it kept coming to my mind. I continued to fight the constant thoughts, but then, I told myself perhaps this was exactly what was supposed to be happening, and I immediately, began to write everything that had come to me where my book was concerned! It was a very incredible experience. Unfortunately, I never spoke to the intuitive again, but it was certainly worth the time!

It had been about three weeks since my experience with the intuitive, when something just as amazing happened. During my recovery from my shoulder surgery, I would frequently go to a Starbucks in the area to work on this writing. Do you believe in coincidence? I don't. What I'm about to share with you may be called many things, but coincidence it is not. As I was on my way to Starbucks to get my daily writing in for a few hours, I drove around running a few errands beforehand and remained on hold with the IRS for one hour and twenty-nine minutes. As I sat outside Starbucks, still on hold, I noticed a gentleman get out of an older, but nice convertible BMW 3 series. Although short in stature, he walked with such big purpose that he caught my attention immediately. His attire was right on point for business casual, and he had all the necessary accessories you are taught to have when you do business. His shoes were in like new condition, in addition he wore quality jeans with what appeared to be a custom-tailored blazer and was complete with a nice watch. I'm almost certain there was a Mont Blanc pen in his breast pocket! As he got closer to the door, we made brief eye contact and spoke just as he walked in. A few minutes later, he emerged out the door with a young man who I would later find out was 25 years old. They walked past where I sat and sat just behind me where they happen to be close enough for me to hear their conversation. I first thought they might be there to discuss social media marketing, based on how the conversation started. This was an area I was trying to learn more about as well, so as I continued holding for the IRS, I took one of my ear plugs out so I could hear a little better. Then, I started hearing more of the conversation. As I listened, it was as though he knew I was listening, and he told the young man before him to watch as he said everything that had been on my mind for the last few years, to prove to him that he was an intuitive or medium of some sort. At this point, I preceded to reach in my backpack to grab the first pen and pad I could get my hands on to take as many notes as I possibly could (but not look like I was). Finally, after about 20 minutes, it began to get a little chilly, and I needed to go to the rest room. As I stood up, the gentleman stood up with a sense of urgency as though he knew he wanted to catch me before I left. Clearly, the energy had been flowing from the moment we spoke to one another almost thirty minutes prior.

    I admitted that I'd been listening to their

conversation from the moment they sat down, so much that I really felt as if I stole from him. It was like sneaking into a seminar of one of the best motivational speakers/business coaches/life coaches, that people paid hundreds of dollars per ticket to hear, and I got an earful absolutely free of charge! After laughing briefly, he extended his hand and introduced himself. It turns out his name was Anthony Barkley, but he was better known as Coach Tony. I assured him, I would be fine waiting for them to finish.

About fifteen minutes later, he came and sat down with me, and the most amazing conversation began to take place. Although I stood a bit taller than Coach Tony, all I could think as I listened closely still assessing things, was that this dude could play a big part of me becoming the me I knew I was supposed to be! Everything he talked about was either something I had done before, presently working on doing, or aspired to do. I would learn there was a dollar amount attached to being able to work with him, and it wasn't a small number. Many thoughts ran through my head as I was trying to decide how I would come up with the money. In addition to bills, I had people I needed to payback. Then, I thought about two things that helped me make my decision.

First, I thought about a quote Coach read to me earlier in our conversation from the former CEO of Google that says, "Every successful person has a coach or consultant - I have one." Secondly, I remember reading a book a long time ago that asked the question: What would you do if you found out today that your son (because I have three boys), or closest loved one needed to have a lifesaving surgery or it was certain they would die, and it was up to you to come up with $20,000 in the next two weeks. How hard would you work to get that money?

Well, for me, it wasn't any of my sons' lives on the line (fortunately), but it was my own, metaphorically speaking. You see, many of us "entrepreneurs" have many things right. We have the skill, intelligence, and talent as well, but at the end of the day, it's like the one variable that makes the difference between that legendary basketball player known in the neighborhood park versus the legendary basketball player who went on to have a successful career in the NBA. It's a coach!

During the three month period I worked with Coach Tony, I learned many valuable things, but the biggest thing I gained from this relationship was he helped restore my self-confidence. There was really no price that can be put on my own personal confidence. As an entrepreneur, I experienced many things over time that began to cause me to second guess myself. Not only was my confidence built, this experience was also like a mental work out as well. This is because when you decide to work with a coach, you must become coachable. You must also humble yourself and be a good listener. I'll give you an example. If you are speaking with someone who is supposed to be very intelligent, and they speak of a specific quote from an author, and it just so happens that you are familiar with that quote and author, your initial thought is to inform them that you are familiar with that quote as well as that author. We often want to do this to let that person know that you have read that same book and that you are on the same level as they are. However, to be a good student or coachable, it would be in your best interest to simply listen and be silent. Things like this may sound easy, but when you get to a certain place in life, it sometimes becomes more important to show your own level of intelligence, than it is to simply listen and learn. Many of the things Coach shared with me, I knew or heard before, but I made a deal with myself to listen and learn. This was indeed a very big accomplishment for me on a personal level. I did so well during this time humbling myself that he had the impression that I was very quiet, laid back, and soft spoken. I was simply making myself coachable.

18

How Much is Your Freedom Worth to You?

I knew when I had my rotator cuff surgery on my right shoulder, that eventually I would need to have the same surgery on my left. Fortunately, I was a lot better prepared this time. I've had Aflac supplemental insurance ever since I experienced being out of work before for three months and not having any real income in 2012. I also made sure all my other responsibilities were all current, to allow me to be as stress free as possible during my recovery time. To my surprise, my recovery was fantastic! I never experienced any pain what so ever, and after a few months, I was due to return to work. Even after all of the preparation I'd gone through to make sure my financial responsibilities were in order, there was one thing I did not consider. I never actually thought that there could be any psychological repercussions after not working for such a length of time. It was as if I were a slave who was set free and had the opportunity to experience and enjoy freedom, and suddenly, I was captured and returned back to slavery and back to the plantation. After having a small sample of what being free was like, not to mention seeing it up close and personal through the life of one of my best friends, Ray, I knew I had to find a way to free myself and find a way to truly begin to live life and not merely exist. It became clear to me that it was my time to make such a decision. It was at that time I had to ask myself, *how much was my freedom worth to me?*

    I knew, as I returned to work, that I could no longer spend my precious time standing behind a chair. I knew the days of me doing hair were about to be over. There was a time when doing hair was my passion and also created real purpose in my life. It wasn't work for me at all. I was simply excited to see what each day in the salon would have to offer. It was always fun, but now it had become clear to me what my purpose was at this point of my life. I just had to figure out how I could free myself and give myself a chance to live life.

    After figuring out what income I would need to create to sustain this new journey, I needed to find a way to generate about $4500 monthly more than my salon would generate. Certainly, my freedom was worth far more than $4500 a month, and that didn't stand a chance of standing between me and my freedom.

I believe that once you identify your purpose in life, you are no longer a part of the money chase. When your purpose improves the lives of others, the money will begin to seek you out. One of the things I learned from Coach Tony was that sometimes it becomes necessary to "burn all bridges that lead to retreat." For me, this meant first announcing my retirement from working in my salon. Secondly, I needed to fill my space in the salon, and my friend Harold was still the number one person on my list. It just so happened that the timing was right this time, and he decided to come on board. Next, getting laser focused on fulfilling my present purpose in life was an absolute must. It had been many years that I'd spoken about being a Motivational Conversationalist as well as becoming an author, but I kept expecting things to be perfect before I could make such a transition. I knew the time was now, as I realized that things will never be perfect, and the timing would never be right to make such a transition. Time itself is by far the most valuable thing we are blessed to have and should never be taken for granted.

19

I Have Everything I Need, to Succeed

Just as we reached our one-year anniversary at The Salon Café', two things happened that had a tremendous impact on me. I unofficially retired. Although I used the term retire, I will forever be connected to this incredible industry of the cosmetic arts, and I hope to continue to inspire future stylists for a long time. Part of my plan to transition to greater things was to join my former business coach in the financial services. After working with him closely for several months, I learned many things about having the proper insurances and investments to allow a person to retire having a good quality of life, while they are still relatively young. I'd already decided a long time ago to use my 30 years of experience in the cosmetic arts to benefit others in their pursuit of having a successful career and being able to incorporate financial planning into the conversation seemed like the perfect fit. As I began to study the state simulator for insurance testing, it immediately took me back to my high school years of standardize test. I previously mentioned how I wasn't a very good student then, and not much seemed to have changed where taking tests were concerned.

In the beginning, I passed the first two chapters of eleven, relatively unstressed. The third chapter, however, took me almost four and a half hours, only to pass the first half of the chapter test. To think I had to pass eight more chapter tests, then take the actual state exam of one hundred multiple choice questions and pass with an 80% or higher to earn my license gave me pause. I really needed to consider if I wanted this bad enough to invest the necessary time involved.

While contemplating the financial service decision, seemingly out of nowhere, my dad passed away. He'd recently been in the hospital for about a week just before his 82nd birthday, and he certainly had age appropriate health issues, but he was hanging in there. I'd spoken to him just the day before, and he told me he wasn't feeling well. I told him to get some rest, and I'd check on him the next day. He laughed, said "Insha Allah" (God willing), and hung up the phone. That would be the last time I would speak with my dad.

His Janazah (Islamic funeral service) was everything he would have hoped for and more.

As my oldest son Scotty, myself, and two other gentlemen lowered my father into his grave, it caused me to greatly reflect on many things he'd said to me over the years, as well as things I have personally learned from my own experiences. Among many things, I could clearly see us shooting basketball in the back yard when I was around 16. He stood at the top of the key and made 30 jump shots in a row, that he never let me forget! While shooting, he told me about many things he wished he had done. Passionate yet stern, he expressed that I should try everything I thought I could do well, and even some things that I didn't do well. What he wanted more than anything was for me to not live my life with regrets about the things I wished I had done. He always said, "life is like a blink of an eye." It's very odd that, that moment would be one of the strongest on my mind the day of his burial. He was the best example of a man striving to serve the Creator.

After my father's passing, I reexamined my life. I didn't want to spend my life chasing money as I had done in the past. I wanted to focus on passion, things that were important to me beyond material things, and serving others. The insurance exam no longer was important. I didn't want to spend time studying for it. Although I know it's a multi-million-dollar industry, and important for people to understand, it wasn't my passion. I only became excited about it as I could feel my coach's excitement. I realized I had all of the components to be where I aspired. I simply had to put them together in the right way. I began to understand on an even greater level, what the title of this book *Trust The Process, Embrace The Journey* was all about. I started to align all the things I wanted to do, beginning with speaking engagements that included cosmetology schools, barber schools, as well as at-risk inner-city youth, and young adults. I knew that everything I'd experienced was for me to share with others. I'd also started an apparel brand a few years prior called Bondseye Apparel. I put it on hold, but I realized it was the perfect complement to my motivational speaking and my new salon café concept, as I needed to make sure the stylist would remain happy, and not feel abandoned since I wouldn't be there working daily.

When it was all said and done, I made the decision to free myself and go for my dreams! This was just the starting point of a new life, but there would be many more things I would do from this point moving forward.

Epilogue

From my many lessons, I would encourage you to take chances in life. Believe in your visions and follow your deepest passions and dreams. It took me a long time to decide to do the many things I'm now doing, but I realize this was the journey I was to have to shape me into the man I am today. I used to consume myself with what people might say, what they may think, and allowed that to hold me back at certain points. I now, clearly understand that when you are called home, back to the Creator, you go alone, and all the naysayers matter not. I imagine the day we meet God he shows you what your life was supposed to be like on a huge movielike screen, based on all the gifts He put inside you when He created you. He probably then shows you how many of those gifts you actually used, and how many you never even tried to explore. I'm sure there are so many gifts inside me that I have yet discovered, but I'm going to do my best to tap into as many as I possibly can before my last day arrives. I encourage you to do the same!

Trust the Journey Embrace the Process